135 PILOT

PASSPORT TO ADVENTURE

BY

TONY BOYD PRIEST

135 PILOT

PASSPORT TO ADVENTURE

Copyright © 2022 by TONY BOYD PRIEST

First Publication:

Published in the United States of America
Published by
ATC PUBLISHING
P.O. Box 127, Senoia, Georgia 30276

ISBN: 978-1-7362222-6-3

Although this is a non-fiction book, some names may be
incorrect and some elements may not be verifiable.
However, all flight records and logbook entries are original
and correct.

135 Charter Pilot ... can mean

This

Or

This!

But the View!!!!!

'Rare Air' at FL450 (45,000 Feet)

Dedicated to

All CFI'S and Aviation Students

We need You!!!
As a Future Professional
Commercial Pilot

In hopes that some of my story will reveal to you some aspects of choosing General Aviation as a Flying Career or as an Avenue to Expedite Your getting aboard an Airline Carrier.

Regardless,

You'll never run out of stories to tell!

TABLE OF CONTENTS

Do You Want To Be a

Part 135 Charter Pilot?

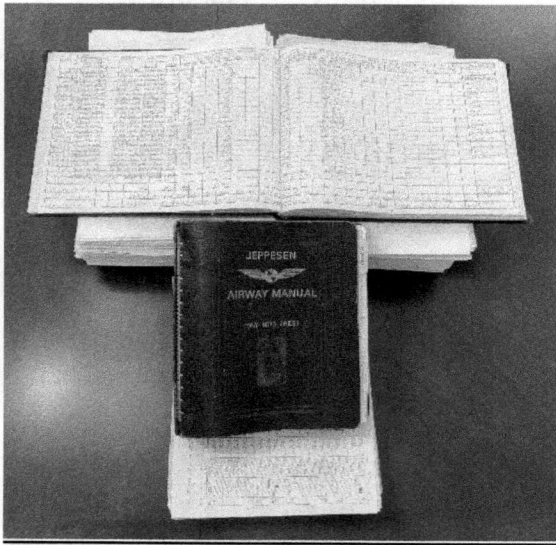

Hopefully some of the Paths I followed and some of the Experiences hidden inside those hours will assist your looking into this challenging and exciting career!

Keep good logs and Company Docs as Backup!

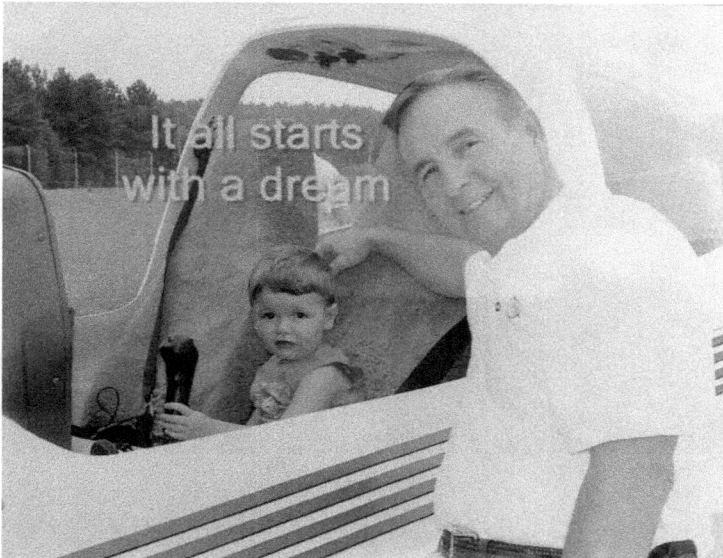

It all starts with a dream

Super Cubs to Private Jets

THE RIGHT STUFF?
OR
JUST THE RIGHT ATTITUDE!

YOUR ATTITUDE
DETERMINES ALTITUDE!

You Start Here...

Tony and CFI Leonard Weekly with 'Snoopy' just before a Commercial License Training flight.

"DON'T THINK OF YOURSELF AS THE 'SMOOTHEST'
DANCER ON THE FLOOR.

ABOUT THE TIME YOU BELIEVE <u>YOU</u> ARE, THAT'S WHEN
SOMETHING CAN AND POSSIBLY WILL HAPPEN.

JUST <u>BE</u> A VERY SMOOTH DANCER
ALL THE TIME!"

TONY BOYD PRIEST

Just an analogy of course. Meaning… Be accurate, smooth, on your target altitude, not 50 feet off!

On the Localizer needle, <u>not left or right</u>…

FORWARD

In writing this book, I've included occasional excerpts from previous books which I felt compelled to repeat as it pertained to a particular safety issue.

My total 29,000+ Hours includes time in several Geographic areas so I feel I have a lot to offer if you're interested in looking North, South, East or West.

As a 5,000+ Hour Flight Instructor, I've experienced a lot of instructional items as well which may appear or possibly be repeated in various sections.

32 years Part 135 experience includes 8 years as Chief Pilot - 2 years as Director of Operations, - 7 years Check Airman – Several Type Ratings – Citation CE 510 Part 135 Instructor - U.S.F.S., O.A.S., D.O.E. and Clearances into several Military Bases.

~

The main purpose of this book is for you to get an idea of some of the various aspects of becoming and flying safely as an On-Demand Charter Pilot or possibly a Corporate Pilot.

My plan is not to repeat all the regulations, technical materials, or details of 135 operational aspects but to present a window into the life of just one Pilot's long career and to present items learned, with a view of possible paradigms in the field <u>you may experience</u>!

CHAPTER 1

THE RIGHT STUFF OR JUST 'STUFF'

Everyone has a different story as to what motivated their thinking about becoming an Aviator.

Some say you have to be born with it and maybe that's true.

However, my definition of 'Stuff' is the ability for one to be Persistent, Consistent and Flexible in your life circumstances.

You may have to reinvent yourself several times to climb into the left seat of a Single Pilot Jet and mix it up with the best of the best.

All I know is that I was interested in flying the first time I looked up and saw an airplane. Even now, it is still fascinating for me to watch an aircraft fly.

Some Inspiration at a very young age.

Lawrence Rainwater, B25, U.S.N. Pacific 1942

Lawrence Rainwater (My Uncle), U.S.N. Pacific 1942
(The only time I knew of a B-25 on an Aircraft Carrier was just before Doolittle's Raid on Tokyo, Japan. If you notice the Sailors' 'Lean' as they're underway in rough seas.)

This picture hung on my Grandfather's wall for years and inspired me at a very young age. It somehow let me know it was ok to dream and that anything is possible, even Flying Airplanes!

Message... Place a visual Slogan or Picture in plain view of your daily routines. Also Place a Picture of your <u>next</u> aircraft to Conquer on your wall!

If you're already a Pilot with Sons or Daughters with aspirations to fly airplanes, you might place a picture somewhere for them as well!

When you're moving along in various aircraft and if the aircraft has a Complicated Panel or complicated systems, you should place a life size panel somewhere in Site of your everyday travels! No need to wait until you walk into the door of Flight Safety, Simu-Flite or one of the other Sim Schools!

On that note, it's very helpful to know the Aircraft and Avionics quite well <u>before walking in that door</u>.

The Why? Why would you want to pursue an On-Demand Charter Position?

On Demand Charter Services may encompass something new almost daily. You may never know where you're heading this week or the next.

After 675 <u>Different</u> Airports as Pilot in Command (Listed in Chapter 11) with 16,437 Landings believe me, that's been a lot of diverse Flight Plans and Challenges.

That alone can be a challenge for some along with Weather, Terrain, Equipment, ATC, your Capabilities and Personal Limitations. ("Man has to know his Limitations"- Clint Eastwood...)

Who you're flying can be interesting at times. May be a Head of State, an Actor, a Baseball Player, a Band, and in Medivacs can be a Preemie Baby, a Heart Victim, or could include a Human Organ pickup in Taos, New Mexico heading to Phoenix, Arizona for urgent Transplant.

I can admit it may be more comfortable to fly a daily route with cargo or passengers.

However, the satisfaction of serving individual people directly, sometimes saving a life, can be a very rewarding position to be in.

Visiting all different parts of the Country or Countries, meeting and becoming friends with your various Medical & Science Teams, Doctors, Crewmembers, Passengers and Local Folks can add a certain quality of life for sure.

Your flying can be quite colorful on occasion in that mixing in with local folks on occasion can give you insight on their local cultures. Leaving the U.S. is not necessary to find different Cultures as there's quite a variety within the Lower 48 states!

I've had both great flights and wonderful and amazing memories flying in the U.S. and several other Countries.

Sometimes you are 'full boat' with a Family, sometimes you have one Lady in a Suit carrying a Briefcase from Miami to New York. She's the only passenger on your B400A Jet aircraft (and she's not talking).

Or, you have a pickup of 8 passengers at midnight at a small base somewhere in Kentucky. You get there and discover they're all dressed in black wet suits with scuba gear (not the tanks) and obviously headed somewhere other than their first destination airport.

(I picked them up at a small base in Kentucky and dropped them off at a small South Florida airport. They were met by two unmarked helicopters and left before I could finish my post flight inspection. No one provided any information.) At the time our company had all our Military Base Clearances.

Every Medevac has a story. With more than 350 missions I've seen pretty much everything of course. Those can be the most rewarding of all. Using your skills Saving Lives is an honorable position to be in.

Anyway, that is somewhat of a short summation of the Why?

GETTING HIRED

To join this elite group of Pilots, first, you have to get hired!

Keep your flying Clean, no regulation bending by showing off to your 'friends' etc. Be a conservative Pilot. Err over on the green side, not the red. In order to climb into that Jet it's a good plan to stay alive all during your training and years working toward that goal!

Remember, a knowledgeable someone has to accept your Resume and your History which hopefully doesn't have any reports of Accidents or Violations. If there's an accident hopefully it was unavoidable and not caused by doing something dumb.

Your looks - dress, demeanor, should be 'Clean Cut'...

Have a serious 'Take Charge' kind of attitude when flying.

(I've been told I have quite a different demeanor in the Cockpit than my normal. – Socially I'm fairly easy going.)

Take charge by having a serious 'Take Charge' kind of attitude in your aircraft.

How do you get there?... With Many Hours of Study! Hours of training and actual Flight Experience of course.

Your P.O.I. (Principal Operations Inspector) or FAA Examiner, or your Check Airman appreciate an Aire of Confidence especially if you can back it up with your Knowledge and Skill!

MY BACKGROUND

Pilots come from all types of varied backgrounds, cultures, and all levels of society.

However, I believe it is important to present some background on myself and possibly reveal a profile of at least one type of person that would choose Aviation as a lifetime career.

I believe it's important to know a little about what drives a person, develops their attitudes, and causes them to end up where they do. Every person has a story. For mine, I'd like to back up a bit.

My story begins way back on the farm in Sharpsburg, Georgia...

Here goes:

I was a crazy little kid, well behaved, though a real dreamer. I was pretty smart in school, I guess, in that most of the time I was in the top of my class, interested in just about every subject. I was raised on the farm and attended Newnan High School in guess where, Newnan, Georgia. I was a good friend of and graduated with Lewis Gizzard (a rather famous Georgia writer), on the track team, in the National Beta Club, and President of the Future Farmers of America. (I actually won a Blue Ribbon at the Georgia State Fair for an excellent Black Angus Steer I raised.)

A lot of wonderful people influenced my thinking in school of course, but three stand out in my memory. Mr. Evans, our principal in his talk at graduation: "When I was a child I spoke as a child, I understood as a child, I thought as a child: but when I became a man, I put away childish things." (First Corinthians 13:11): Mr. Worley, my Agriculture Teacher, taught me a lot about leadership and getting a job done. "Fellas', you've got to Plan your work and Work your plan!"

One of the most influential was Mr. Smith, my English and Literature Teacher. Mr. Smith was unique in this part of the Country in the 60's. He was an immaculate dresser, always totally neat in appearance, a meticulous speaker. He was soft spoken, a gentle person throughout. Although he was an intellectual person, he had a sense of humor and was easy to talk to. His classes were always interesting and challenging, but most of all, I believe his personality and demeanor let me know that it was okay to be a different sort of man than I'd been brought up around.

If you're still out there guys, "Thank You" for your help and inspiration. And, of course, I am very thankful for all my Teachers, Professors, and Instructors throughout my life and career.

During my early years, there was little connection with my life to Aviation. I was generally discouraged from being a dreamer by almost everyone around me and was reprimanded for watching airplanes when I was supposed to be working. And, although flying airplanes seemed really far out to my family, I have to say my Mom and step-Dad were always there for me through the years.

I had always dreamed of flying, both with and without an aircraft. I've heard that if you dream of flying, you're actually trying to escape from something. I don't totally agree with that, but there may be some truth to it. My ambition to fly has been simply a yearning for learning more, seeing more, and experiencing more of life. I just knew there was more to life than I could see around me. I loved my home, my family, and my friends, but I had to go see for myself. Thank God we live in a Country that allows you to Change your life, to Expand your mind, to be More, and to test your own metal. The Army has it right - BE ALL THAT YOU CAN BE!!

Although I spoke of the Army, after High School, in July, 1964, I joined the Navy, tested and qualified to become part of a special company called the 'Peach State' Company.

Every one of us was from some town in Georgia, and scored high enough to be selected. We attended boot camp together in San Diego; most made it through, some didn't. Boot camp was probably the first life changing event in my life. When you're always around your family, friends and the surroundings that you grew up with, your life may remain pretty much the same. Boot Camp was like a severe slap on the face with an ice-cold, wet towel. Your attitude changes immediately. You grow or die (not literally of course). You choose to survive, you grow up inside, you learn, you move ahead, you Graduate.

After Boot Camp, I qualified for an "A" School and chose Electronics' Technician School located on Treasure Island near San Francisco. However, after a few months, I decided I'd had enough of that and volunteered for Sea Duty. Shortly, I was assigned to the U.S.S. Vammen, a Navy Destroyer on which I spent two years. That was a totally incredible experience and another story!

After that tour, I received orders to Port Hueneme, California to join up with MCB 3 in support of the 3rd Marine Division. At that time I was qualified Helm, Lee-Helm on the Destroyer and also in almost every small craft the Navy had.

My first questioning remark was, "What the heck kind of Boat is that?" The answer was, "Son, that's not a boat, you're headed inland somewhere between Hue and Phu Bai, South Vietnam!"

MCB III (Mobile Construction Battalion Three, commonly called "Sea Bees" (or "Fighting Sea Bees" for us John Wayne fans) was already In-Country, meaning already on duty in Vietnam. (Since his name has come up, I need to tell you more of my personal profile, John Wayne was one of my greatest heroes, falling somewhere in a line of heroes after Jesus and my Dad.)

After a couple of months of training and preparation at Port Hueneme, I was shipped down to Camp Pendleton, San Onofre near San Diego. There our unit went through three weeks of Survival and Combat training with the Marines.

Shortly after, I found myself strapped into a Delta flight headed to Da Nang, South Vietnam.

What a shift of paradigm to have a hostess offer you tea or coffee enroute, then having the Pilot perform a radical go around at Da Nang under heavy rocket and mortar fire.

After circling the scene for some time, we eventually landed with full military deplaning, making it to the bunkers and ditches. I spent my first night laying in one of the ditches with my sea bag laying on me as additional mortars pelted the area.

For you that know a little about the war, you know 1967-68 was not a good time to be anywhere in Vietnam. Well, the next morning, all of us picked up our orders and directions to get to our companies. Only two of us were sent on our way to catch up with MCB 3.

A few hours later, we caught a spot on a truck convoy headed up Highway 1 to Phu Bai.

After a good day's ride in the country, we found out the Bees were not in Phu Bai, but were at their new location, a new Combat Base called Gia Le located just a few miles from the Old Imperial Capital City of Hue. Shortly we caught another ride and finally made it into camp.

The Combat Base consisted of 120 Sea-Bees, a segment of the 3rd Marine Division, a group from the 101st Airborne, plus an Air Cavalry squadron of nine helicopters.

Here's <u>one</u> of the stories.

We'd seen a lot of action in the preceding months, lost several Comrades, however, nothing was like what unfolded on us January 30, 1968.

I'd just been relieved from my 8 – 12 PM watch, made it over to my hooch and sat down on the stairs.

Glancing toward Hue I could see what I thought was their TET (Lunar New Year) Celebration with fireworks flying into the night sky.

I made the comment to myself, 'Boy those guys really like to celebrate their New Year', when suddenly I could see tracers flying in all directions in the distance. 'That's not good!'

With my 45, Grenades on my belt and M16 in hand I tore through the door of our Hooch alerting the guys to the situation.

I ran over to our alarm system which was outside nearby and realized it was inoperative. It was blowing air but no warning horn. Evidently a round had already penetrated our warning net.

We all began running from one hooch to another, in one door and out the other screaming "Incoming! Incoming!"

After about my fifth hooch all hell broke loose as they began hitting our camp with everything they had - mortars, rockets and artillery.

It seems that somehow more than 50,000 Viet Cong and North Vietnamese Regulars had infiltrated into our area.

If you're military, ever heard your Lieutenant screaming "Fix Bayonets!!!" over and over as he ran along your perimeter line?

We did and prepared to fight an unseen enemy hand to hand if necessary. Still Absolute Total Darkness except for Muzzle Flashes and Explosions.

Yes, I along with everyone else did plenty that night, ducking dodging diving and firing at shadowy images as they penetrated our wire (ropes and ladders) and were running through our camp, firing at will and throwing satchel charges into bunkers and buildings. Our perimeter had been broken in 2 areas.

I had several near misses, got blown into a bunker, drove a jeep at '50' miles per hour backwards away from a blown-up burning building, even relieved our exhausted mortar crews for a time.

Soon, our camp buildings began lighting up with fires starting all around the camp. Sure enough, the enemy had been effective with their satchel charge suicide missions. We were taking them out quickly but they had done and some were still doing a lot of damage. Don't remember sleeping for a week!

By 0300 eight of our Air Calvary helicopters had been shot down over Hue. The 9th managed to crash land back on base. The 'Captain' had been shot. As we assisted him to a stretcher, he told us that it was total insanity over Hue and he was concerned about the others...

Accompanied by a Corpsman we hauled him down to the LZ for a flight out on the next Medevac.

(I plan to write more about all that in a future book.)

Just painting some of my background.)

If you can imagine, Vietnam may have left me an 'Adrenalin addict'. But whether or not that's the case, I've got to thank the military as they clenched my interest in Aviation. I believe that's where it all started for me. Riding in and observing every kind of flying machine in action really got me going.

Yes, after Tet, some of us came home where everything around us was different, seemed plastic, frivolous. We'd changed for sure. But, after you've become a Veteran of a War and Mortal Combat, you have to decide whether to cost yourself fifty or sixty years of a viable, productive and fulfilling life or let that experience end all hope you can ever have it.

I believe we all have PTSD to some degree, some worse than others. BUT, the way I thought and continue to think about it is why not use the same focus and controls you gave in 'Mortal Combat' to control the 'Enemy' within you.

Enough of that... Just wanted you and others to know if I could do it,

You Can Do It!

If you need a place to kick out some adrenalin, head to the Airport and get to work on

Your Pilot's License!

"If you decide to spread your wings and break the surly bonds of your own life's gravity, be prepared for an ultimate high, but also be prepared for an occasional ultimate low.

When you find yourself in such a low, a 'Valley', Learn from it, Focus your Mental Energy into Improving and Build on your Future Plans to accomplish them.

In that Valley is where your Character is Built and believe me, If I could do it, You Can Do It"!

Tony Boyd Priest

IF YOU DECIDE TO STAY STATUS QUO,

REMEMBER

*'YOUR **COMFORT ZONE'** MAY BE A BEAUTIFUL PLACE,
HOWEVER <u>NOTHING GROWS THERE!</u>*

LET'S GO FLYING!

Your track may not be anything like the one I followed.

However, it's the trail I stayed on working my way 'Faster' and 'Higher' on a continuing basis finally getting to Single Pilot Jet and Single Pilot Jet Instructor, flight at 45,000 feet, and highest ground speed just about possible in a G.A. Aircraft at 634 Knots (about 730 M.P.H.) with a little jet stream push of course on a Dallas to Atlanta Leg.

I'll only be skimming the surface of course as a long multi-faceted career like mine would make a pretty thick book.

Even if you catch only one or two helpful items or find one of Captain Tony's Rules or Suggestions to be worth following, I believe your time will be well invested.

There's some local History and some stories that may actually be very entertaining.

Also, you'll probably see areas where I discuss a lot of safety items as, again...

Your Remaining alive will have a lot to do with the length of your career.

You may also feel my frustration about why Pilots are continuing to make the same mistakes that hundreds of Pilots have died from.

Is it from Gaps in Training, or simply a Human Factor, or possibly a combination of both?

Here goes...

CHAPTER 2

CALIFORNIA BASE

Although I was born and raised a Georgia boy, I ended up in Southern California for several years.

If you take up your pursuit of an Aviation Career, you probably will have to move around the Country or possibly even out of the Country.

Also there may be times early on when a non-aviation job may be necessary just to pay the bills. That's especially true if you have a young Family.

I attended Mt. San Antonio College located in Walnut, California. The college had and still does have a great Commercial Aviation Department along with some awesome Instructors.

At that time, United Airlines had an Internship Program which I participated in. (Not sure if that is still active with the college.) After passing the flight Engineer Written Tests and completing the program, I actually got some Flight Engineer experience and some Stick Time in the DC 8!

The amazing Captain Bill Arnott worked closely with the college and was a definite inspiration for all of us.

His Motto mentioned occasionally was to

"Aim and Climb Higher"

'Captain William S. Arnott was a United Airlines test Pilot and Line Pilot who flew nearly every aircraft in United's fleet.

Bill joined United in 1946 and worked tirelessly to instill in United's newest Pilots a sense of history and accomplishment. Bill had a passion to preserve United's past for future employees.' -*United Airlines Historical Foundation*

Thank you Captain Bill Arnott!

During and after College I completed the majority of my flight training program at Pomona Valley Aviation at Brackett Field in LaVerne, California.

'PVA' was one of the best and most active Flight Schools in California at the time.

Early in my career the school as well as the location were very good in that I had real world mountain training as well as intense instrument training.

Simultaneously, I worked full time for Southern California Edison, a power company as by this time I had a small family to support. That job helped pay my way but limited my flight training to primarily weekends.

However, during that time, I attained all my License and Ratings except ATP (Airline Transport Pilot) which would come later on after 1,500 hours flying time.

Through our training years, most of us have an Instructor who's very important and generally the most influential to us.

Although I had other Instructors along the way, Leonard Weekley, CFII -MEI, was my personal Friend and Mentor during those five years. He was an easy going individual which came through in his instructional techniques and his mannerisms. He was extremely knowledgeable and motivational, with complete insight into problem areas and how to solve them. Not only was he one of the best flight instructors I've ever had, but he became a good friend till the end. I owe him the greatest thanks for the thrill of my first solo flight at El Monte Airport., El Monte, California. For you who have experienced that, you know it's something you will never forget.

After attaining my Commercial License, I joined Leonard in the Civil Air Patrol and eventually became a C.A.P. Captain. (Not only are you helping others, possibly saving lives, you're Building Time!)

We had C172's and C182's available along with some of us getting time in our T6 Texan.

We were successful in many of our searches as well.

If you can get involved it's a great organization to help others and to gain experience for sure. And No, we did not practice strafing trains or trucks on the Freeways.

Little did I know how far I would be able to go from there!

During my training for my Commercial and Instrument Ratings, I was also privileged to complete an Aerobatic Course in our 7KCAB Citabria.

(I highly recommend taking a good Aerobatic Course somewhere along the way as it might save your Bacon sometime in your Career. It did mine more than once.)

With my Flight Training evenings and most weekends, along with additional hours accumulated with the C.A.P., I was closer to 500 hours and had completed my Commercial, Instrument, Multi-Engine, CFI, CFI-II and CFI-MEI License and Ratings.

This took me about 5 years from my First Solo Flight while holding a full-time job.

Persistence... Setting Goals... One step at a time.

You of course can do this much faster as it will all depend on your personal circumstances!

Somewhere at about this point in life examining their Career Goals, one has to make decisions about solid income and 'security' vs their Core Values.

I had enjoyed my time with Southern Cal Edison. All my Friends and Co-Workers thought I must be crazy to even think about leaving such a solid company. I already had 6 years with them, had moved up several positions and income, and had received a couple of appreciation letters for accomplishments and innovation suggestions, etc.

(Of course several of those friends went on to spend their 20, 30 or 40 years there and 'retired' long, long ago. Just not sure if they're still excited about their life.)

(Historically back a bit) In my case, it could be the same Core Values instilled in my early years of wanting to do more, and to be more, that I left a normal life of what everybody else was doing at home (some college, some jobs) my Cabinet Shop job at the time and went into the Navy.

For the same reason, although qualified and landing an Electronics Technician A School, spent a couple of months there, and soon realized 4 walls was not where I wanted to be. Then Volunteered for Sea Duty and spent 2 years on a Navy Destroyer. Then volunteered to join up with the Navy Sea Bees and head to South Vietnam.

However, I survived all that, went back to a normal job back at home working for Bell Telephone Company in Atlanta. That one took me about a year to escape.

Then back to California and Southern California Edison to remain there for those years, attending mostly night classes at 'MT. SAC' and as mentioned did most of my flight training nights and weekends.

OK. The Soulful Challenges and Rewards I discovered in Aviation I <u>absolutely</u> could not find anywhere else!

If you're having trouble making the jump, you'll have to really <u>analyze your own Core Values and Life Requirements</u>.

After making a short story long, after completing my License and Ratings I gave notice to my Power Company Job and began Instructing Full Time.

MY CLIMB TO ALTITUDE BEGAN

CHAPTER 3

GEORGIA BASE

After attaining most of my Ratings, I finally made it back to my home state and found an Airport close to my home.

Falcon Field near Peachtree City, Georgia had a 3,000-foot runway. There was a maintenance facility, AeroSpec, run by an awesome couple, Wayne and Joyce Hutcheson.

In the same building was Joe Black Avionics and Andy Anderson Aircraft Interior Company. There was very little flight training going on at the time.

I was referred to and found a Delta Pilot with a Beechcraft Sport who was willing to lease it to me by the hour.

It was slow go at first but eventually I added a Cherokee 140 and soon became Falcon Flying Club.

Building from there, I continued to take on additional aircraft and eventually had another Instructor working. About a year along I was approached by Hangar One in Atlanta to lease us two new Beechcraft Sundowners. I already had a Beechcraft Sport on line so this seemed like a good way to go.

Along with their aircraft, they offered me to attend Beech Craft's first ever Beech Club Pro School in Wichita Kansas. I attended, graduated and a few weeks later had our Grand Opening of the first and only Beech Aero Club in Georgia.

Along with this, Hangar One offered to lease us any aircraft we might need and they did including a new E-55 Baron! At that time, we already had a B-55 Baron but our Club had continued to grow with some great folks flying daily.

Through the next year or two, I became a pretty good promoter for our Club and Airport and came up with several ideas.

One of the first was to set up a live display 'show and tell' for Peachtree City Residents and to catch traffic along Hwy 16 between Newnan GA and Griffin GA and possibly capture attention from some Atlanta folks. (No Internet, no Websites in those days! Just had to get creative.)

How did it get there? Well, I first drove by car various routes from the Airport to downtown Peachtree City and when I found a route pretty much free of obstacles, contacted the local Peachtree City Police and explained my goal.

After some scrutiny about the viability of the situation, we were approved!

The City had to temporarily lay down several Roadside Signs, then stand them back up of course.

I had full Police Escort for my Live Taxi effort in the BeechCraft Sierra from the Airport to Downtown to set up in the Peachtree City Bank Parking Lot!

Yes. Mr. Floy Farr himself (one of the Founding Fathers of Peachtree City) approved us as well!

Mr. Joel Cowan, another Founder and early developer of Peachtree City, may have influenced his decision as Joel was an Active Club Member. Also Mr. Hollis Harris', President of Delta Airlines, son was one of my Students at Falcon and a Member as well. Both were great Friends of Mr. Farr.

So to make a long story short, we at least for the weekend, had quite a display in the middle of town!

Absolutely cannot imagine trying that today.

Here comes the next thing. Most thought... What now?

Some Background - All during my early training in California, the Brackett Field Airport arranged for several Air Shows.

We had everything from the antics of a Piper Cub, to Art Scholl, Skip Volk and other Icons such as Bob Hoover along with aircraft Demos of Military Aviation which always brought lots of folks to the Airport.

Along with that knowledge, about Spring 1977 I came up with and discussed the possibility with Wayne and Joyce Hutcheson of AeroSpec.

With their help and after a meeting with the Clayton County Kiwanis Club, we managed to kick off the First Annual 'Falcon Field Air Show' in Peachtree City, Georgia.

I was amazed that over 3,000 people attended the first day with more the next.

Wing walker Donna Behrendt thrilled the Peachtree City's Falcon Field with her crowd at an air show held last weekend in aerobatic stunts. (Photos By Al Mullins)

largest circulation newspapers on the Southside...

Fayette And Southside **Sun**

A crowd covers the hillside as they enjoy the show. (Photo By Gary Webster)

Daring-Do Of Air Performers Thrills Crowd

The Objects
of Kiwanis
International

Certificate of

Appreciation

Presented to

Tony Priest

by the

Kiwanis Club Clayton County

*In recognition of your sincere and unselfish con-
tribution toward the success of our 1st Annual Kiwanis
Airshow Fund Raising Project.*

Dated this 20TH day of July, 19 77

Ed Downey
PRESIDENT

Roger C. Will.s

Did get a little recognition for my part but more importantly watched the dynamics of our Flying Club and our Airport begin to develop in our small town!

(If Flight Instruction is your immediate goal, learn to be proactive in attaining and keeping Students. Perhaps not at this level in today's world but utilize all avenues possible to stay busy.)

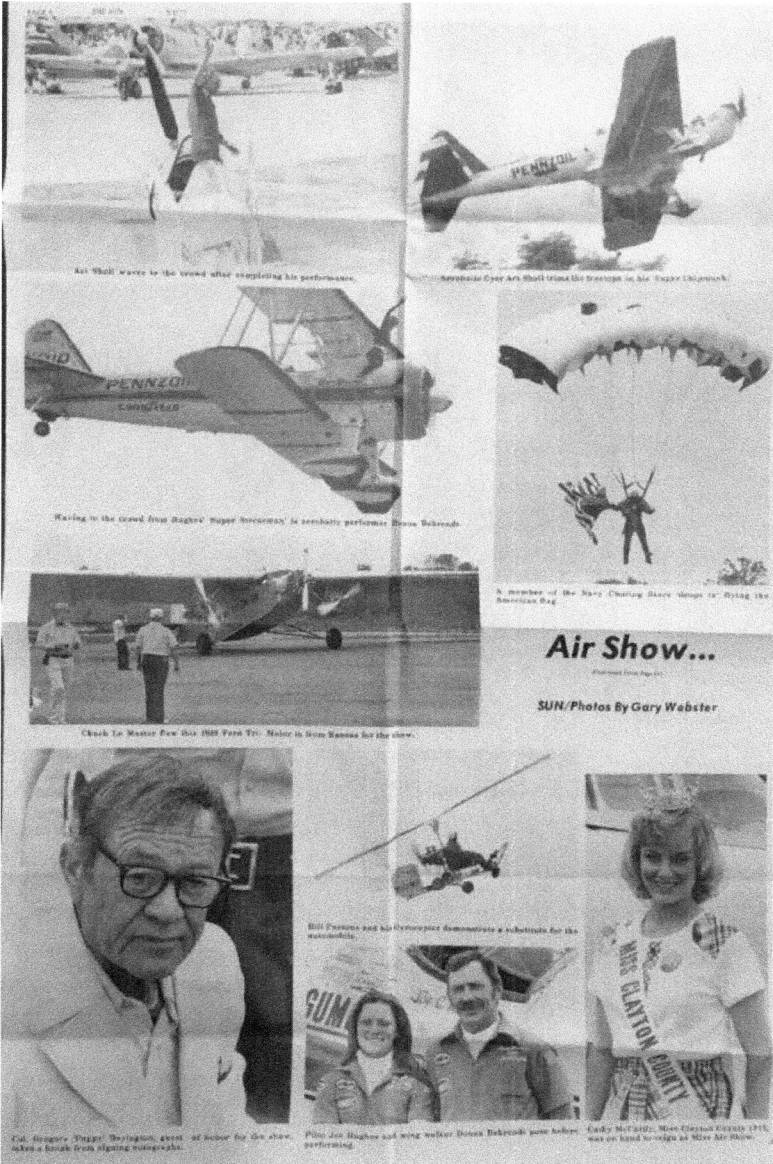

Air Show...

Continued from Page 00

SUN/Photos By Gary Webster

Retired Colonel 'Pappy' Boyington, was our 'Guest of Honor' at our Airshow, possibly the first in the Atlanta area.

Gregory 'Pappy' Boyington was a Marine Corp Ace, who led the Black Sheep Squadron in the Pacific, was a Medal of Honor winner and Navy Cross Recipient and after finally being greatly outnumbered, was shot down himself, survived and was picked up by a Japanese Submarine, then spent 1 ½ years as a Prisoner of War!

As our Airshow opened, he flew in, climbed out of the cockpit, and spoke about 20 minutes to hundreds of people.

Later on he was sitting at a table near our Flight Club Display, speaking with folks about his Life, flying in the Pacific and Signing his new book 'BAA BAA Black Sheep'.

I've always been respectful, interested and open to Words of Wisdom from those gone before us in the Aviation World and later got my chance to spend some personal time with him which I'll never forget.

He was a tremendous person to be around and had quite a few stories to tell. Here's a memorable tidbit from one of our conversations.

"Tony, you know I love Flying and Airshows. Don't mind talking with folks. But..., my problem is that every time I meet someone new, like when I climb out of a cockpit or step into a room, the younger people all look disappointed. They're all expecting Robert Conrad! Not an Old Leathery Gentleman like myself."

Yes, you could see the years on his face as well as the hours of mortal combat and hard life experiences that possibly only another war veteran could really appreciate. I certainly did.

I could see his point. However, we all have to remember the Aviation Industry was built on the shoulders of Giants such as 'Pappy' Boyington!! .... A Tribute.

https://www.youtube.com/watch?v=-0r0E5D83BI

Well the old 'Falcon Field Airshow' continues to this day and has grown to be quite an event.

From the Falcon Field Airshow, to Great Georgia Airshow, and now Atlanta Air Show

https://airshowatlanta.com/

I really enjoyed working and flying out of Falcon Field for those years, built a lot of friendships, introduced a lot of young folks to Aviation, launched a lot of new Pilots, including several Airline Pilots, and had some really great Fly-Aways.

Some of our Fly Away activities had been Ski Trips, Beach Trips such as Hilton Head S.C., Flights to N.C. Mountains, Biltmore House and Gardens, Bahamas and to many Airports for Airshows or to simply have a meal together. We visited ATC Facilities, had Guest Speakers, Barbeques and so much more. What a great time!

However, The Iranian Revolution began in 1979 and was followed by a deep Recession. Beginning 1980 things really began to slow down for our Club, Flight School and the Airport in general.

Kinda' scary as it reads something like some of the events of today's world!

As the Flight Schedule began to have blank pages, I had to begin dropping off some of our leased aircraft. Then later, once again supplemented my income with an evening shift job.

(This happened more than once during my Flight Instructor and early 135 Pilot career so try to build into Good Investments and Savings Account(s) to buffer unexpected financial Reversals!)

I continued on with my factory night job along with occasional flights. Regretfully, eventually we had to close our Club entirely.

However, I had completed my ATP during the period and surpassed my required hours for 135 IFR.

[Under FAR 135.243 For VFR Flying, you will need your Commercial / Instrument and be qualified to fly the category and class rating of the aircraft being flown. You will need 500 hours total time to include 100 hours cross-country and 25 hours logged night time.

For IFR, you'll need 1,200 hours of flight time as a Pilot, 500 hours of cross country, 100 hours of night and 75 hours of actual or simulated instrument with 50 hours in actual flight.]

(Might check the Regs if reading this a year or two down the road.)

So, it can be done through Flight Instructing! Just takes a while.

On the historical 'downside', I'd spent 4 years in the Military, then began flight training some years later once back in California. Between College and Flight Time on weekends, it took me several more years more or less to complete and attain all my ratings. Then building time put me way out of the age brackets Delta or any of the large Carriers were hiring at the time.

However, I continued to press on toward a possible airline career. After completing my ATP at 1500+ hours I applied at several Airlines with no results, but later on got a personal recommendation from Hollis Harris, President of Delta Airlines whom I'd visited in his Office. <u>I was 33!</u>

<u>(I was told from another source that Delta had not hired anyone over 25 for years.)</u>

He sent me over to A.S.A. a local Commuter at the time who were flying three DHC-6 Twin Otter aircraft. After completing the interview, I was offered a First Officer position and a date to begin class.

However!!! When it came to Salary... No way could I afford to work there with my Family and a Home now.

I thanked everyone but withdrew my application and began looking elsewhere.

If, however you are offered and <u>can afford</u> to make the jump, Do it by All Means!

CHAPTER 4

BACK TO CALIFORNIA

Reach out. Move ... Again! for better Income with my growing Family, better equipment, and a chance to fly Part 135.

Late 1979, my Wife, whose Mom was in California, had already begun to persuade me to return to the area. It was June, 1980 when I finally ran across a Flight Instructor Ad in Trade-a-Plane, and later found myself at Big Bear Lake in California.

That really interested me as I was familiar with the Airport and area.

After speaking with Steve on the phone, Big Bear Aviation, I found he was a part 135 operator as well as a Flight School.

That turned out to be a really great job, my first great adventure in aviation. I loved the people, the fresh mountain air, and the challenges of flying out of a High-Altitude Airport.

BIG BEAR AVIATION –

I arrived and was met at the San Bernardino Airport by the awesome Steve and Linda Wallace. Both turned out to be great folks to work with. Thank you both greatly for the opportunity!

Things went quite well, took a thorough Check Ride with Steve, and got the job.

He reminded me how hazardous flying in California can be especially flying in these mountains.

I began Instructing and stayed pretty busy flying the hours working with several students.

Steve was flying a Conquest II for a corporation and eventually handed over most flight instruction to me.

I gained a lot of good friends and soon pretty much managed the operation.

A lot happened during my time living and working at 7,000 feet. Stayed alive and built quite some experience.

I've included a few stories hopefully to relate how to <u>stay alive</u> in those mountains.

It was a challenge at times especially in winter months as there were plenty of snow storms to deal with. For instance, one morning following a heavy snow I arrived at the Airport and could only see the tails of our aircraft. Lots of careful shoveling required that day!

Between storms, winter flying was generally good for performance however many times there was a trade out with high winds out of the southeast which came right down the valley.

Summers could be quite challenging as well. Primarily dealing with Density Altitude. I'm sure you've read all about it and probably experienced the lack of aircraft performance yourself.

DENSITY ALTITUDE ALERT! –

For example, one of our training aircraft was a Cessna 152.

One morning after calculating Density Altitude, performance charts and considering a stable headwind, I decided it was safe to fly. However, even with ½ tanks, I knew it was somewhat on the wire so to speak.

Westerly Wind was 15 – 20 knots right down the runway.

With a nice Tailwind for taxi, we easily made it to the run-up area.

After completing our checklist with a thorough runup, we pulled onto the runway, eased into full throttle holding the brakes and leaned for best power. All looked good and "Let's go."

My Student released the brakes and... - We didn't move! That 20-knot headwind was holding us in position!

Then, the wheels began turning... one revolution, then another. "Hey Bill, I've got an idea. Let's keep rolling except taxi back to the ramp. Fly a little earlier tomorrow."

He seemed quite relieved as we taxied back to our tie down and of course utilized substantially more power than we used taxiing downwind.

From that point I applied a little more margin of error computing Density Altitude and Performance! **(Just because the Aircraft Flight Manual says you're within parameters, use caution. If it's an older aircraft, those numbers when newly tested may not apply today.)** Needless to say we didn't do a whole lot of training in that aircraft during the warmest summer months.

GROUND EFFECT SAVE

Another friend in Big Bear purchased a 1949 Cessna 140A (85 HP), flew it in one evening and the next day decided to take it out toward the desert. (I'd previously warned him about the D.A. problem and buying a low horsepower aircraft.)

Although his flight was early morning, he had his share of troubles it seems.

"Selling my 140 Tony," he mentioned a couple of days later.

"Took off East yesterday but spent about 30 minutes just trying to stay alive in Ground Effect. Don't think I ever got above 30 or 40 feet. Finally made it back to the runway!"

He did keep it for a while afterwards but flew with a much lower fuel level and limited his flights to early morning or evening.

Ground effect there can be a blessing or a trap. For instance, if taking off westbound, with a good breeze but a warm temperature you might find your takeoff reasonable with the aid of ground effect.

Then, you leave the runway area, then over the fence and now the shoreline. Now you're low and over the Lake getting the full attention of boaters and fishermen. The good thing is you're over the lake with no obstacles. The bad thing is you're over a lake unable to climb out! No Thermals to help there!

A cautious turnaround and still low but back over land 'hoping' for some thermal activity.

('Hope' of course is not a word that should be in a Pilot's vocabulary. Other terms – "maybe' or 'might' make it," or "probably be alright," etc.)

However, one could consider flying straight ahead, fly in ground effect over the lake, clear the Dam and dive down the valley.

I would only do something like that if it was an Emergency. Factors such as turbulence past the dam in the rugged valley may play a significant role in your airborne capabilities. Your planned out could become a 'coffin corner' just as well.

However, I usually demonstrated a flight down the 'Low' route to my students on a clear, still day to use as an emergency 'Out' if needed. The terrain drops rapidly but in turbulent conditions, could be a scary ride down.

Out to the East we had the desert down below as long as you could make it a few miles and over a few hills.

We taught our students as many 'Outs' as possible utilizing various scenarios. Hopefully that's still a practice today.

If you live in a mountainous area, it's a very good plan to work out as <u>many</u> scenarios as possible.

'What would I do if I had'

- a 'rough engine'
- 'loss of an engine single or multi'
- 'oil on windshield'
- 'loss of turbo-charger'
- 'sudden loss of visibility'
- 'caught in a blind canyon'
- 'extreme turbulence'

Speaking of turbulence here's a quick note about traveling Westbound from Big Bear Lake.

TURBULENCE –

One of the rules learned in a hurry was if the winds at the Airport were 25+ out of the east and right down the runway... Take off on the east runway of course - You're Airborne quickly... Great Groundspeed on your downwind departure... Totally smooth air... No problem... Until... You begin your descent into the L.A. Basin.

In my early days in Big Bear, on one of those days with strong easterly winds, I began my descent down the mountain a little too soon.

When those winds are funneling down the valley, they can accelerate, then take a tumble off the mountain further out and in a big way.

Thought I was well clear of the mountain side and any roll clouds, however encountered the shock of Extreme turbulence right after I began my descent.

First was a severe downdraft followed by a severe pitch up. Airspeed was all over the place. Turbulence was severe. Totally out of control. Just tried to maintain attitude and power as nothing else worked... I went through several gut-wrenching gyrations ... Until, finally it let loose and I was back in smoother air. That was a really bad ride for sure.

From that point I quickly learned to climb up and stay at altitude for several miles from the mountain side to remain above the expected turbulence. Worked well after that. Still turbulent but nothing like flying into a rotor. (I was not a Mountain flying Genius in my early days.)

PIPER APACHE INCIDENT –

This incident occurred on a Multi-Engine training flight over the mountains on a clear day.

Anyone that knows the Piper Apache with its approximate 5,000 Foot Single-Engine Service Ceiling is probably wondering what an Apache was doing in Big Bear. The Runway is at 6,752 feet! And surrounded by 8,500 ft mountains.

Well, it was a private owner's aircraft newly based there. He'd wisely requested additional training in the mountains.

I reluctantly took on the job knowing to <u>treat the aircraft like a single</u>. Lose an engine... Land... Somewhere.

We of course went down to the desert areas east to work on our single engine maneuvers.

This particular day all had gone well with my student and the aircraft. We were returning to Big Bear and as we crossed the eastern mountain ridge at 9,000 feet, I decided to demonstrate the single engine performance at altitude. Just so he would know how the aircraft performed on one engine in case it happened coming or going.

I pulled back the right engine smoothly and he went through his normal engine out checks and went to his best single engine speed. We were discussing his 500 FPM rate of descent and taking care of his 'good' engine.

As we crossed the ridge, I began bringing up his right engine back to normal when...

"Bob... We may have a problem with the left." As I pointed to the temp increasing on the very engine we were discussing!

Glancing back, I noticed smoke trailing from the left side!

Back to the instruments I could see the oil pressure dropping rapidly.

"My Aircraft," I stated.

"Looks like we have a problem as I eased the throttle on the right back to normal. Your temp is climbing on the left, trailing a little smoke."

I quickly shut down the left engine and feathered the prop.

He glanced back over his left shoulder to see the smoke increasing.

I continued to bring up power on the right keeping it in parameters. The problem was we were now below the ridge behind us and exactly between the Big Bear Lake Dam and the Runway both at 6,752 feet.

At takeoff the winds were out of the west. Using my best judgment decided with the winds, we had a better chance of making the runway to our left than landing short of the dam in the cold water.

Now at best power on the right engine we had a substantial descent rate. About 500 FPM.

I had the student call May Day on Unicom frequency. I knew we could not reach anyone else due to the terrain surrounding us. (I continued to secure the engine for landing.) He got the Airport and advised them of our situation and to have fire and rescue standing by.

As we continued to drop below the surrounding terrain we heard "Fire Department's been called. On their way! Good Luck boys!"

"Thanks Dewey," I called <u>calmly</u> recognizing his voice. (Hey, my Student's listening and watching everything.) Dewey Richardson was a really great guy and Airport Manager. I knew he would be taking care of business on the ground.

As there would be no go-around, I knew to play it to the absolute best of my ability.

In our continuous descent toward the Airport and a modified downwind, we turned a 180 to a short final for Runway 26, lined up and deployed the landing gear and flaps at last minute. That was only 3 - 4 minutes into our emergency! Yes, writing these couple of paragraphs took at least 3 – 4 minutes! … Obviously we made it.

In my ultimate focus, squeaked it on – NBJF (no brag. just fact). Both were quite relieved to say the least and taxied in to the ramp.

As there was no smoke, just a cold engine, we sat for a minute going over what had just happened while somewhat catching our breath as well.

"Let's take a look at that engine," I mentioned.

"We climbed out and began looking around the engine. Lots of oil but no other apparent fire damage.

"I've got my tools in the hangar," Bob mentioned as he turned and walked briskly on his way. He returned with some tools and we proceeded to remove the cowling… There it was… A broken oil line.

We were continuing to look over the engine when we heard the sirens in the distance coming our way.

As they arrived, all were quite relieved to see a couple of Pilots standing in front of their plane. (That was not a usual outcome for them!) I thanked all the guys for coming out so quickly.

Later, I thanked my Guardian Angel for Guidance and Control and my Instructors, especially CFI Leonard Weekly, for his Great Mountain and Multi-Training.

Look for your 'Outs' in various scenarios and Practice Them on Good VFR Days.)

I continued with Big Bear Aviation for some time and had great success with my Students.

Later on and after a check ride with the FAA, had experienced some great Charter Flights.

However, as a Pilot, I of course wanted to continue growing in my career.

Following a flight one afternoon, had a good opportunity proposed to me by another operator on the field. Thus, I reluctantly gave notice.

NEXT STEP: 135 Full Time Charter Pilot

Stepping on out and getting into full time Air Charter is not too hard of a stretch. (You're used to Study, Aircraft Systems, Regulations and the Airmen's Information Manual for a start.) 135 just gets to be a little more restrictive.

Plus, I felt it would be ok as, if needed, I could always fall back on Flight Instructing.

(Be sure to Keep your CFI Current no matter what career category you fill.)

HOWEVER, Be Prepared...

From This... 1 Page in 1920.

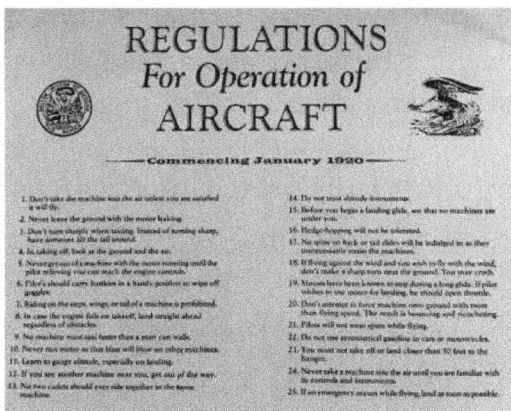

To This... 1,176 Pages in 2022.

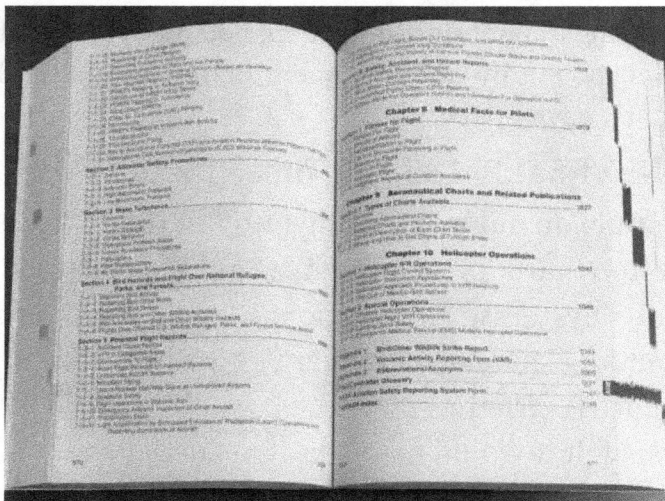

Federal Aviation Regulations / Aeronautical
Information Manual

'You will have to know and be able to explain pretty much everything within this manual at this point. Part 135 does require some additional study!'

MOUNTAIN AIR – FLIGHT INSTRUCTOR, CHARTER PILOT

All was going well so far in my new mountain surroundings when I was approached on the ramp by another operator on the field. Mr. George Benton of Mountain Air Service who finally persuaded me to come over to his Part 135 Company and fly his newly acquired Cessna 401, a twin-engine Cabin Class aircraft.

Although Big Bear Aviation had occasional 135 Flights, my work primarily had been Flight Training and managing the Flight School. Here before me was an opportunity for serious Part 135 Flights and a Scheduled Mail Run 5 days a week.

Owners George and Irene were another husband-and-wife team and were really great folks.

Although we had some occasional work in the 401, we primarily flew charters in a Turbo Arrow, a Cherokee Six with a Ray Jay Turbo Charger, a Piper Saratoga and various other singles.

My primary weekly duties were flying Bank Mail daily with pickups and deliveries at El Monte, Van Nuys, Hollywood Burbank, Santa Monica, then over LAX to Orange County then Riverside and back to Big Bear. Those were the days when paper checks were flown around to various Banks of course.

You can imagine the complexity with LA Approach Control especially in IFR weather which was almost daily.

That's ok as you can and do get used to the fast action.

Most of the time takeoff from Big Bear was VFR and you could expect either IFR or marginal VFR due to fog and smog down below

AIRPORT INFORMATION TODAY

(All that was some time back of course. Today there's over a hundred aircraft based at Big Bear and the Airport is complete with a Restaurant and plenty of parking.

As always, it's a good practice to make yourself familiar with accepted procedures at a new Airport especially one at 7,000 feet and to fly up with someone who's familiar the first time.

From the West inbound, make your approach over the south side of the valley and over the ski slopes at 9,500 feet and for outbound fly out across the lake at or below 8,500 feet.

The Pattern is 8,000 feet with Right Traffic for RW 8 and Left Traffic for RW 26. RW 26 is the calm wind runway however as in most uncontrolled Airports don't count on that being the gospel.

One helpful action to take inbound here or at any non-towered Airport, is to light up your aircraft. Turn the landing lights on, Yes even at noon on a clear day. Many aircraft tend to blend in with the environment especially against snow covered terrain. Also, you may encounter high altitude Raptors (There are Eagles in the San Bernardino Mountains.) or other birds around the area and it's been proven that Birds will generally turn away from a Landing Light but may not turn away from an aircraft.

Another much appreciated action is when inbound on an IFR flight plan, if in total VFR conditions, cancel as soon as possible. That frees up airspace for the controller and may allow another aircraft to depart IFR. That may also give you more time to evaluate the local traffic.

By the way, if departing to an IFR destination in the Basin, the Controller may not appreciate a pop up coming off the mountain and may not want to work with you so file your flight plan.

ATC and Radar are generally not available below about 9000 feet so check the ODP for night or marginal weather VFR or IFR.

OK. You say you're clear and blue and 22. Why check the ODP at any Airport.... Remember your **'What if's'**. There are several scenarios that may put you in an IFR situation on takeoff and climb.

Immediate condensation inside your aircraft, smoke from a possible fire in the engine, a broken oil line throwing oil, or how about this one, a swarm of bees or other insects creating green goo on your now opaque windshield. That happened to me.

It's good to have something to fall back on should that occur.

A professionally flying Pilot does.

We fly expecting something to go wrong and are surprised when everything goes right. Not the other way around as <u>regretfully</u> too many do today.

'GRID BLACKOUT' AT BIG BEAR –

(I left this story in due to 'Learning from Experience'.)

On another trip, I'd dropped off my passengers in Las Vegas and was returning to Big Bear. It was a dark summer night with a high dense overcast.

Although desert area, the terrain west of Las Vegas can be deceptive and deserves respect for coming in or going out. There's not much lighting along some pretty high hills.

Going either way, high is not a bad idea. Check the topography carefully.

The particular trip home was uneventful but very dark.

I'd had a long day, anxious to get home and was glad to see the lights of Big Bear coming into view.

I crossed the blacked-out ridges below me and now had full view of the Big Bear Valley.

The lights looked great as I began my descent to the Airport....

Then it appeared that a section of the city had experienced somewhat of a blackout. I noted to myself the darkened area, 'Looks like the town of Fawnskin has lost lights.'

Then I observed another section go into a blackout. It appeared the entire North West section of town was losing power.

Then, as the blackness began to eat up the lights below me...

Whoa! I rotated to climb adding full throttle! Pulling now for the best angle of climb! Still dark below me I angled slightly left toward some distant city lights.

Suddenly, everything below me was lights!

You bet. I was visually descending into a mountain ridge.

I may have been only a few seconds from impact.

Perhaps sometimes Pilots get to fly a long time just because they're lucky.

Always Be Wary of possible illusions while around mountainous terrain, especially at night!

Learning from that experience, at night or in poor visibility to this day I descend only over the lights of a mountain valley Airport..., never while approaching the valley.

The same goes for departing with a darkened-out horizon. Climb overhead the lights then when positive you're clear of all your surrounding terrain go on your way.

Even with today's GPS and TAWES systems, some push the envelope for one reason or the other and fly right into the terrain. "Yeah, it's all red but I know this section is not that high. Been through here many times." – Last words.

Or, if flying up a valley at night or in poor visibility depending on your TAWS System. Might not want to bet your life the system will get you through.

I've personally experienced two iPad failures and two GPS failures. which brings us back to charts. Always have backup charts even if you and your aircraft are wired to the gills. Sometimes it's hard to protect your iPad from direct sunlight. At what temperature will your iPad shut down? Your Janitrol heater fails at 12,000 or higher. You're stuck on top due to icing below. How much cold can your iPad battery carry on with?)

Through the years in Big Bear, I'd gained a lot of hours and a ton of experience both as Flight Instructor, and as a Charter Pilot.

The mountain flying there had been challenging but rewarding as well.

I met a lot of people and made a lot of close and wonderful friends.

However, 'There he goes again folks!'

Chapter 5

Las Vegas, Nevada

This was a step up for me career wise and financially. Reluctantly, I left life in the beautiful Big Bear Valley Mountains for a life in the big city. Luckily, my wife was as excited as I was about moving... again.

Thus, here comes another Chapter in my book and in the life of a Charter Pilot!

You want to fly 135, be prepared for change. –

Working from Big Bear, I had taken many charter flights to Las Vegas.

While standing by for one of my Charter customers at North Las Vegas Airport, I wandered around checking out some other operations.

One in particular caught my attention as I spotted a Seneca II and III, a Lance plus a Cessna 402 and Aero Star 650P on their ramp.

I walked into the front office and spoke to Lisa, a very friendly lady at their small counter.

I found out the company was primarily a freight operation with several bank contracts. They occasionally had passenger trips as well as Medevacs. Sounded quite interesting to me so mentioned I was open for a Pilot's position if she knew of anything.

She said "Possibly" and went into the back to speak to their Chief Pilot.

John Dunahee came out and in a very cautious manner asked me to come on back.

As usual, I had a short Resume with me and presented him with my experience so far.

He thought it looked pretty good but had several resumes to look over and would get back.

I thanked him for the consideration and headed back to the Strip.

Two weeks later he called, "Tony, would you be interested in starting out with our night mail run? It's actually not a night job but you primarily would be flying at night. Depart Las Vegas at 0500 with a stop in Tonopah, arrive about 0715 in Reno, spend the day at our apartment, then head out about 1900 back to Vegas."

Sounded simple enough, "Sounds fine John. I can be there in two weeks."

A NOTE ON GETTING HIRED…

One of the things that's always worked for me is to simply walk in, show your face.

However be prepared. Investigate the company and equipment they utilize. Review the Personnel and Culture' of the Company… In other words – Do your homework! Find out Who's Who,

Then – Look Sharp, Rested, and simply walk in with Resume in hand and ask for 'Thomas' (the Chief Pilot).

I've had the Chief Pilot of a very large 135 Company, say Hello, glance through my Resume, then show me a 3-inch stack of Resumes that had been mailed in.

"Tony, it's good to see you in person. I simply do not have time to review and call all these folks.

Well, here you are, nice resume, qualified, current 135.

When can you get started?"

Just sayin'. May not always work but worth a try!

Well, Training went well at Interstate Air service. Of course, passed another check ride with the FAA, then flew a couple of training missions.

Well, somewhere along the way, I found out that two previous Pilots assigned the Tonopah, Reno Route had hit the mountain adjacent to Las Vegas.

The VOR Airway turned and they didn't. Dark Night – No lights on the mountainside of course.

ALWAYS KNOW WHERE YOU ARE AT ALL TIMES.

On that note: Having gained quite a bit of mountain experience flying throughout California, I eventually came up with a system that's a comfort to have, especially single engine.

Day or night especially in single engine aircraft and especially at night – Expect a sudden weather change or Engine Problem.

Leave Yourself an Out... How?

In general, fly the ridges or over the highest points in the mountains which gives you a much better chance to descend safely in any case where required. That is unless the terrain tops are above your normal operating altitudes.

Then plan to fly on the windward side of the ridges and peaks to avoid the worst turbulence plus you'll get great speed with a lesser power setting. Why?... Because of the general uplift currents, Trim nose down and Go Faster!

Plan and plot on your VFR Chart your Mountain Escape Routes. Yes, On your Chart! Your Chart should be on your lap or close by for sure. Avionics may help – TAWS, I Pads, etc.... However not that handy if everything turns Red! Or if they Go Blank due to overheat, battery, or some other glitch. If they are working, they may not differentiate the best terrain for an approach to an emergency landing or show you your best Glide Path to get to an old Forestry strip or flat field.

It's not a good plan to try figuring out what you're going to do 'after' the engine suddenly dies or if you've iced up due to 'unforecast' conditions.

A Dead Stick landing following your Planned Escape Route –
Congratulations You and Your Passengers are Alive.

ICED UP IN THE SIERRA NEVADA'S -

While flying the night mail from Las Vegas to Reno, I encountered a few severe ice situations.

Occasionally when we had lighter loads we flew the Piper Lance, a single engine aircraft. Lots of stories to come but first focus is on that element.

It was the middle of winter and yes right over the mountains, I encountered <u>unforecast</u> Heavy Snow. Normally it's not a problem except this day, Ice began to build on the Lance leading edges.

I flew for a few minutes expecting to get out of it however it became worse and began to build more rapidly.

I asked for higher altitude hoping to get on top, however with the ice building I was not able to climb any higher.

I still had a mile or two visibility however was now losing the mountain peaks due to snow building over the rocky faced mountains.

Now I discovered that with full power I was slowing and could not maintain altitude. My windshield was pretty much opaque now with a small area to view through at the bottom with my Defrost Heat at full blast. I told ATC my intentions, cancelled IFR and continued down. In that case I <u>had</u> to continue down with very marginal VFR.

I'd already looked on my Chart for the planned 'Out' course plotted (4.3 NM from the VOR on the 037 Radial) and turned just beyond the VOR on a heading to intercept. I intercepted and flew the Radial now in continuous descent passing 7,000 feet well below the mountain peaks. Now hoping to break out shortly and if not could continue my descent following altitudes planned on my Chart.

Yes, following one of my preplanned 'Out' routes I had arrived in one of the valleys. The conditions were warmer and I began shedding ice. Also, now with much better visibility and ice rapidly peeling off, I was able to continue VFR to my destination, Reno.

When you survive those kinds of situations, you can put another experience into your flight bag.

ANOTHER ENGINE OUT -

Here's another event where one of our new Pilots had a very close call with an Engine Out and where pre-planning may have saved his life.

A few months into my job at Interstate I was promoted to Chief Pilot. One of my responsibilities was to train new Pilots and familiarize them with the routes and destinations.

Don was one of our first new Pilots.

On our initial training flight to Reno as we were flying along, he asked "What are the yellow lines on your chart departing right and left of your course."

As I explained, "If night or IFR along this route, these pre-planned 'outs' are courses I can fly to get to a landing spot while avoiding the higher terrain.

The marked routes included VOR radials and DME Fixes to verify those 'Outs' and identify the best landing spots.

He seemed to understand and thought it was really a good idea.

Eventually he was assigned the route on a regular basis and I moved on flying more On-Demand Charters and Medevacs.

It was a couple of months later when I arrived back at home base, I saw Don walking rapidly toward me. Stopped and gave me a great smiling handshake, "You won't believe what happened last night."

"You know those routes I copied and drew into my charts, Well, I did lose an engine, picked up the nearest 'Out' route and managed to glide to that old airstrip you'd pointed out during training!

It was dark but had a little moonlight to find the strip!

"Wow, Don! That's amazing. Glad to hear that! Good Job."

"Thanks man! I sure appreciate the advice!

Speaking of single engine in the mountains, I give this tidbit from previous experience to anyone flying in the mountains in a Single Engine aircraft.

Here's the accepted procedure

<u>if you did not plan your outs properly.</u>

'Darn... Engine quit. You're at 12,000 feet over mountains, can't see a thing below except black.

Set up your best glide speed right away, go through your engine out procedure and complete your emergency checklist. Dim the cabin lights and secure the radios you don't need for your MAY DAY calls. You're conserving your battery for flaps.

When you descend into utter darkness and when you think you're getting close to terrain,

TURN ON YOUR LANDING LIGHT.
IF YOU DON'T LIKE WHAT YOU SEE, TURN IT OFF!

Seriously –

Plan and Leave yourself an Out.
Plan your Mountain Escape Routes.

REMEMBER the Dead Stick Route Followed to a Successful
Landing – Dark Mountains...
Escape Routes - Leave Yourself an Out –
Congratulations You're Alive.

The same goes for Multi-Engine. Know your Single Engine Service Ceiling! – Check your weight – Input a discount value according to your aircraft age and condition of your aircraft – Plan your escape routes.

ICE INCIDENT SENECA II –

I was flying back to Las Vegas from Reno in really rough conditions over mountains at night of course. I'd kicked off Auto some time back and had been in icing conditions for about 20 minutes. Checking alternative altitudes, routes, there wasn't much available.

I was stable at 9,000 feet with both engines running smoothly. However, I suddenly went from light continuous ice to moderate. 'Not good.'

As I began to take on more ice, I noticed my airspeed beginning to drop off. I continued to maintain altitude.

After a time, airspeed began to drop more rapidly.

I had checked my 'out' courses ahead by this point in case I was not able to maintain altitude.

Cross checking as airspeed continued to drop off, I observed my pitch angle holding about a normal cruise position. Power settings were normal with smooth engines. (I deducted that with normal cruise power my attitude should have moved more upward. My thought of course, 'What if I'm simply losing my pitot system due to the ice'. However, I still considered my routes to lower terrain and an 'Out' just in case.

My airspeed continued to deteriorate, soon - 100 knots, now drifting toward 90 knots... Then 85 knots, Then 80 knots.

My Pitch Attitude was stable, however, still 'Sweating Bullets' of course. I closely monitored and scanned other instruments. Thinking that if it hadn't stalled at 70 knots with all the ice, there was more than likely a Pitot Tube blockage.

With hand on the throttle, I quietly listened for any stall warning and watched for any burble of the wings. Airspeed continued to fall. Night, windscreen covered. Now Airspeed continued to go into redline for stall but nothing happened.

Airspeed now 60 – now 50 now 40, 30, 20, ZERO!

I was somewhat relieved, however that should never have happened!

Approaching North Las Vegas (VGT) in my descent the Ice continued to dissipate and my airspeed slowly came back to normal.

Of course, a write up for maintenance – Pitot Heat Failure.

St. Elmo's Fire Las Vegas –

Both VOR Indicators FAILED SIMULTANEOUSLY.

Our Mechanic said he'd never heard of that happening.

Well, it did!

Most Pilot's I've shared this with had never seen an incident of Elmo's Fire.

Once again, returning from Reno to Las Vegas I encountered moderate snow – Night in smooth conditions.

The first time I noticed the phenomenon was when a sparkly glow began outside my wingtips.

I'd previously shut off my strobes in the heavy snow.

This continued for about 5 minutes.

Then, I noticed little strings of light moving onto the wing. Mostly white as small strings of lightning but with a sometime blue hue.

There wasn't anything I knew of to correct or change things as the little arcs continued now toward the cockpit.

Flashes like little lightning bolts began in and around the side windows then into the cockpit!

Then, arcs began at the top of the windshield, traveling down the windshield and out the bottom!

Shortly, a complete circuit of a continuous miniature lightning bolt began as it grabbed onto the magnetic compass down the windshield, down to the panel and back up to the compass!

It had created its own continuous loop.

Continuously scanning, I realized both my C.D.I.'s (Course Deviation Indicators) were pegged in the shutoff position. I crosschecked instruments, still on heading, on altitude.

Tried to adjust the needles to verify, neither needle would move. Tried off and on then reset my avionics circuit breakers, all to no avail.

I could not reach ATC for vectors and at this point I was primarily flying a heading. My magnetic compass tested ok as I moved left and right to verify.

My Directional Gyro was working fine.

The one navigation radio I had available was the ADF.

I had on occasion listened to a strong Radio Station in Las Vegas, so I tuned it in. (no NDB Airways nor directional beacons in the vicinity.) Sure enough, I was able to pick up the Las Vegas Station. This seemed totally odd to me as I was working now with a low frequency radio! Didn't make sense but it was working.

Suddenly in conjunction with the ongoing light show there was a sizzling sound with occasional pops.

Now there was a pulse to it as it flowed from my magnetic compass down the windshield, onto the glare shield and airborne back to the compass!

That arc continued to occur and pop about every 10 seconds.

I reached to adjust the ADF when suddenly, fire flew out of my fingertips to the instrument panel.

This was really getting strange... Zero - Zero in moderate snow with all this lightning activity in the cockpit. Now I'm part of it!

I spread my fingers on my right hand, noticed I was glowing and slung my hand toward the right window. Arcs flew from my fingertips to the window! Did that three times.

Totally radical scene. One I'd never witnessed before. A little tense to say the least.

I had the fire extinguisher handy in case something started smoking but none of that occurred.

Then I broke out on top, looked around and noticed I'd passed through a quite tall cumulus buildup. Now I was on top of about a 7,000-foot layer.

The arcing slowed down, then disappeared.

Shortly I noticed my CDI's were alive again and made a slight adjustment to my course.

One for the books I thought. I was very thankful to have obviously come through that unscathed!

My first encounter with Elmo's Fire had lasted about 15 minutes. A Spooky 15 minutes!

Checking around the cockpit, I could find nothing obviously wrong. All instruments and navigation were back to normal.

Our mechanic scrutinized every inch of the panel and cockpit area. Nothing... However, there was a faint smell of hot insulation remaining.

All static wicks were in place; however, he did find one with a somewhat frayed ground wire.

Sometime later I read where a few others had experienced the same phenomenon.

After researching further, 'Elmo's Fire' seems to be an 'electric plasma field causing ionization of the air molecules.'

It was quite a light show. The experience felt other worldly for sure.

Always count and inspect your static wicks and ensure the ground wires are connected and not frayed.

ANOTHER ICE INCIDENT –

When almost every flight for several months includes Ice and Night Flights, it's no wonder things can happen.

Again in the Seneca II, heavily covered with Rime Ice, Night, I once again approached Las Vegas.

I broke out of the overcast at 6,000 feet entering warmer weather and VFR Conditions.

Ice began melting with water streaming off the aircraft. The windshield had totally cleared up. I cycled my De-Ice Boots once more to assist the shedding to get rid of any remaining ice.

As I descended on down to 5,000 (2,000 above the Airport) the aircraft seemed perfectly good to go. Airport in sight, I canceled and entered a wide high left downwind well over the Las Vegas Strip, I utilized my normal routine,

Approach Flaps, Gear speed now, Gear Down. Still a little high…

Considering my above pattern altitude, I selected 25 degrees flaps.

As usual I was hitting my configuration airspeeds close to the top of the mark.

At about midfield on a wide downwind now, still high, I selected Full Flaps…

As they clicked into place, guess what.

I flipped over into a nose down vertical position! Floating, hanging in my belt with the lights of the Las Vegas Strip in my face!

First Thought - **Tail broke off!!!???**

I did what I was trained to do in a severe upset.

Undo What You Just Did!

From this extreme nose down position with Vertical Speed pegged, I performed a normal Stall Recovery,

Full Throttle, **Reduce flaps back to 25 %.**

I began to round out, regained control and leveled the aircraft at about 1,000 feet.

I was over the extensive lights of Las Vegas and attempted to reorient myself to the airport…. Wow… I'm alive!

Searching the extensive lights now, I spotted the runway and continued around for a landing leaving everything exactly the same prior to adding the full flaps!

'A normal recovery worked and I didn't touch any buildings or wires!'

I couldn't speak at this point with my only thought to get this turkey on the ground! Didn't matter as the tower was closed as usual at this hour.

After landing, I climbed out of the airplane, dropped onto the asphalt and dropped a knee.

I Gave extensive Thanks to my Maker.

Shortly, regaining my composure, I began carefully examining my aircraft.

Not one thing wrong or out of place!

I secured the aircraft, grounded it for maintenance and slowly walked to my car.

The next day, maintenance had inspected every detail and could not find anything wrong with the aircraft.

I questioned our mechanics and later everyone I thought would have any idea what had happened.

No one, including at our local FAA Office had any idea.

Until... one day on the Crew Bus in Reno, once again on a wintery day, I began talking with an older Airline Captain and described my Seneca incident.

He thought for a minute and said, Son, you're lucky to be alive.

There's been several fatals' caused by that very thing. You had a **Stabilator Stall**!"

"A what?"

"Although you'd shed all ice you could visibly see, you evidently had some Ice on your Horizontal Stabilizer. You say it was a Seneca with a Stabilator, well that there is your problem."

"When you increased to full flaps, with some left-over tail ice a disruption occurred and the tail stalled!"

"Good thing you did exactly what you did or we wouldn't be sitting here talking!"

"That accident has usually occurred on final when the Pilot selected full flaps. In that case, always fatal as there's not enough room to recover."

I thanked him for the information and passed it on.

'Stabilator Stall' – a new one on me... Piper Seneca or any aircraft with a Stabilator in weather to me dictates utilizing only 25 degrees max flaps. It's a hard call whether to fly at normal airspeed or increase your airspeed in ice as we've all been taught. There's some that say a higher airspeed can actually create more of a problem for the tailplane in general.

Tailplanes generate lift the same as wings, just negative pressure to balance the aircraft. When flaps are extended the downwash air strikes the tailplane at a higher angle of attack than in normal flight. This increases tailplane lift and pushes it closer to its critical angle of attack.

I keep my speed up and simply use less flaps for landings after a flight in icing conditions!

My **'Undo What You Just Did!'** rule applies to many other scenarios. Could apply to several items such as asymmetrical Flaps, Switching to a Contaminated Fuel Tank, Deployment of a single Speed Brake, etc.

That rule saved me more than once!

RENO – Be cautious of wind right down the runway.

Reno Weather – 5,000 overcast with winds right down runway 16 at 45, occasional gust 60. Night of course! Blowing dust on both sides of the runway.

'No problem. I'll be airborne, climb out quickly and head on course'.

The tower cleared me for takeoff, "Out of 8,000, Cleared on course, Maintain 12,000."

I was right. Airborne right away! Steep climb! Beautiful!!!

However, at about 7500 feet MSL, BOOM!!! I encountered Extreme Turbulence!

Teeth shattering jolts hanging in my belt one moment, pulling g's the next. Vertical speed pegged at top, then pegged at bottom! Not fun to be 2,000 feet above the ground with that indication. Airspeed was flipping from 0 to Redline and back to zero knots!

I knew that some of what my out-of-control instruments were showing were radical pressure changes.

I requested a turn back for landing as I worked to control my aircraft with attitude and power only.

The tower cleared me to land.

However, as I approached downwind, my vertical speed was suddenly pegged at the top, but now in smooth air! My altimeter was winding like a fast-moving clock!

Now in smooth conditions, climbing rapidly toward my assigned altitude, I reported the new conditions and requested to continue on course.

Cleared again on course, I almost missed my 12,000 Ft. altitude assignment which I reached in about 2 minutes!

I turned on course and was handed off to Center.

Still in smooth air, I realized I was surfing a Mountain Wave right off Mount Rose!

After fighting to maintain altitude, I requested a block between 10 and 12,000 and headed to Vegas at a tremendous ground speed.

What hadn't entered my 'pea brain' before my departure, was that the winds aloft were out of the West at 70 or 80 knots. The Runway was 160 degrees.

Yes, the Airport winds were right down the valley. The Winds aloft were almost perpendicular at 80 – 90 knots.

Where the two winds met along with rotors off the mountain was where I entered the extreme turbulence.

I was very lucky to have made it out of there!

Wasn't long after, a Navajo Chieftain took off and on climb out encountered a similar condition, rolled inverted, had some structural damage which included a cracked wing spar. The skillful Pilot managed to get it on the ground but the airplane was totaled! He for sure was very lucky to be alive.

Really consider all factors regarding Terrain and Winds Aloft direction and velocities!

My simplified thought pattern of 'not a problem, 'should be able to climb out quickly, some gusts possible', etc. would probably have come out ok in Kansas.

LACK OF O2 AT NIGHT

This could happen to you! Be aware...

I was climbing out of Reno another cold winter night.

Expecting an 'on course' instead received several vectors right after takeoff due to incoming military traffic.

Out of 10,000 feet the controller gave me another turn. I replied and chuckled to myself. Then, another turn, on my way to 11,000. I replied and chuckled louder and complied... Then thought... 'That's not funny!'

It dawned on me... 'Forgot my Mask!'

Slipped it on and after a solid breath, the 'Lights Came ON' so to speak.

Hypoxia was slipping up on me.

I received my final vector toward home, auto on, relaxed and thought about what had just happened.

Had I not caught myself, would I have possibly passed out?

Just a word of caution. I know we Instructors discuss Hypoxia and how the O2 level can drop to +/- 5,000 feet at night, well, it must have been quite low that night!

'Sneaky' Hypoxia... Be careful!

**Always be cautious when flying low, even in the desert.
Always be ready to go on the gauges.**

TONOPAH CLOSE CALL –

Again, a dark moonless night in the desert. IFR Departure.

Just after takeoff I was climbing out over the blackness Cross Checking Instruments, I noticed my Attitude Indicator showing Wings Level but my D.G. Course creeping as in a turn. I had no visual horizon at all, just pitch blackness.

I scanned up to the Magnetic Compass and saw it too was creeping along.

As I moved a little left to stop my turn, I realized my Attitude Indicator was going out.

It's would be one thing if it had straight out failed, however this was a very slow-motion failure that can get you killed low to the ground!

My turn coordinator seemed somewhat questionable as it appeared sluggish so I went to airspeed, magnetic compass and D.G to hold my heading.

That seemed to be working however a little unnerving as the attitude indicator continued to slowly bank further until it finally went to a 90-degree angle.

I'm at low level, zero visibility and from a general instrument panel perspective I was in a roll!

Shortly, I was able to pick up my VOR Radial so now I had three instruments to work from and continued on course.

Needle – Ball – Airspeed! You hear all the time. This time Airspeed – Magnetic Compass – D.G. – now VOR.

Sometimes you have to be creative in your Instrument Flying!

Always, Always, Always!

Scan – Cross Check your Instruments!

If... I didn't have that <u>Habit</u>; I would have simply been a statistic.

In your instrument training, always incorporate partial panel proficiency. With no obvious pitch information as I had, balance your flight regimes by knowing your Power Settings vs Climb, Level Flight, and Descent. Know your rate of turn timed with a clock, etc. and

Remember,
Your instruments tell you what has already happened.
Experience tells you what is going to happen!
Be Smooth
Practice Partial Panel!

Another good habit to have when approaching your destination VFR expecting a Visual approach. Plug in the expected runway's ILS or other IFR Approach in case you might have a sudden loss of visibility. (Remember to always expect or be ready if something should go wrong.)

It may also help you line up on the correct runway in case of Parallel or Angled multiple runways with nearby finals, or near a Coast Line or Mountain range when expecting visually north – south or east west alignment.

Had to say goodbye to my wonderful friends in Tonopah, Lake Tahoe, and the great towns of Las Vegas and Reno.

A good friend I had met in Reno, Jimmy Gibson (Graduated from Georgia Tech) had convinced me I could make a fortune in Alaska. He was already there and having the time of his life.

Well, I had been living my greatest adventure to that point, flying the mail in the Sierras between Las Vegas, Tonopah and Reno with occasional Charters or Medevac flights in the Cessna 402 and even attained some Aero Star time.

From what I'd been through the last few years and with the experience gained I felt ready for Alaska and a new challenge!

So, about two weeks later, my adventurous wife and I packed up our Chevy to the ceiling, sat two wonderful kids in between all the boxes and hit the road.

CHAPTER 6

ALASKA!

The Sierras can be just as unforgiving as much of Alaska and its pretty good training ground for someone wanting to go up to the far North country.

Where you have high terrain, weather, rocks and ice coming together, chances are, it's looking like *Alaska!*

"Experience is like altitude. The more you can draw on the more options you will have to get out of trouble when the time comes. That time will show up, sooner or later, in Alaska."   *Captain Tony Boyd Priest*

I know it's simply a place, however, it's also, still... the 'Last Frontier' so to speak.

I plan to spend a little time in this section so I assume that if you're looking into flying as a Commercial Pilot up there you might want a few details that are not in any book. The Details might save you a lot of grief sometime in the future.

For the most part, you work on your own, have your own thoughts, make your own decisions, however your rewards are many. Friends are solid, somewhat of a feeling I had during my military years.

I began as a Flight Instructor, which shortly slipped right into Part 135.

My first mission there was hauling fish from various Seaside Villages into Anchorage in a Beechcraft Queen Air Converted for Cargo Operations.

Mixed with that there were occasional Cessna 206 and C207 Charter Flights to many destinations.

As the summer ended, the company shut down for the season.

Now I had to get creative if I wanted to stay in Alaska.

After a short time with another operator, decided to start my own company which included forming and operating a Flying Club. Later on, ABA Flying Club, under Arctic Basin Airways, became a Part 135 Company.

(You might want to connect to the following Blogs for some stories and excellent pictures regarding some of our Aero-Club flying in Alaska. Just Click on these two pictures.)

If you're in the Print Book go to 'wannabethere.com' 'Blogs' and look for 'Dawson City, Yukon Territory' and 'Flying the Prince William Sound'. (Flying the Sound was totally never-ending Amazing.) If you're in the Digital Book, simply click on the next two pictures.

Dawson City, Yukon Territory

Tatitlek Village, Prince William Sound, Alaska

Our Flying Club utilized other Carriers on occasion for larger groups. The amazing Roland Suter, Pilot, and Business Entrepreneur set up one of our largest Flights.

For those of you who have a desire to fly in Alaska for a season or for a few years, might take note:

"Alaska is not a good place to build time for low time inexperienced pilots."

An old adage states... 'Experience is the best teacher', however, when it comes to Aviation in Alaska, this is not necessarily true. Other pilot's experiences are extremely valuable, especially if you're teachable and wise. If you're determined to make the journey, read everything you can on the subject and try to find a good mentor who has been around a while. It's better to have flown a few hundred hours before even considering going north. The basic stick and rudder flying has to be a natural trait. It's as simple as that.

Also, it's a good idea to Flight Instruct in Anchorage or Fairbanks for a year or so to learn from those long-time Bush Pilots that want to work on their Instrument Rating or Multi, etc. Learn how they managed to stay alive out there. Then your chances for longer term survival begin to improve. Always be open to learning something from others especially when you're new in their world.

Regretfully some pilots seem to have more guts than technique. Becoming a successful pilot in Alaska is a learned trait that takes time and experience. Learn and master the skills and get to know your own personal limitations.

Plan to take FAA Safety and Survival courses. Know the aircraft you're flying (or flying in) and always be prepared with emergency gear, even on short flights.

Always file company or FAA flight plans.

During my time with ABA as a flight Instructor, I firmly believe I had learned as much from my students as I had taught. Floats, tundra tires and skis were just a part of the diversity in equipment. As far as diversity of the people, well, you've got to be of a different sort just to live in Alaska!

To fly in this vast, wild country, I believe it takes a certain type of person. I found most of my students and pilot friends through the years to be very mission oriented. In other words they were determined to accomplish whatever goal they were assigned or had given themselves.

Not all our students and pilots were macho male types either. We had several females that demonstrated the perseverance it takes to become a pilot in Alaska. Several wonderful ladies such as Bev Holding, Wendy Agen, Susan Metcalf, Dianne Tarrant and others, trained there, did the hard work, overcame their fears and flew cross countries across the Alaska wilderness. All became excellent pilots - Alaska pilots.

As far as being mission oriented, take Susan Metcalf for instance. She was a warm, soft-spoken yet determined College Student who wanted to learn to fly to get out to more of the outlying villages. Her primary goal was to teach Native American kids to swim. Drownings at the time were prevalent throughout Alaska. She wanted to make a difference and I believe she did that.

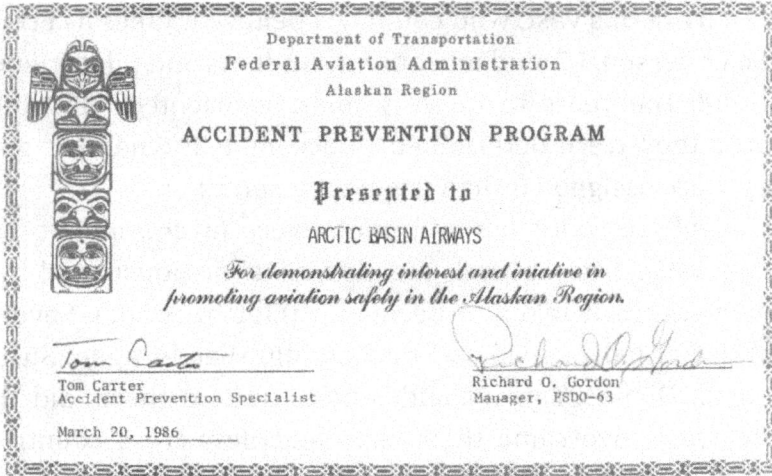

We were building and growing steadily and highly respected by the Alaskan Region FAA.

Throughout a couple of great years at Arctic Basin Airways and ABA Flying Club, we had a lot of students graduate to higher license and ratings and visited a lot of Alaska. Personally, I had gained a lot of experience through flying with and being around a lot of highly experienced Bush Pilots along with 135 Operations.

Here it goes again.

Somewhere near the end of summer in 1986 we heard news about a possible oil price crash. However, it didn't hit home until one Saturday morning when only a couple of students showed up. I personally had nothing scheduled but came in during the day to check on things.

'Nothing in the morning at all, hmmm... At least Buck's got a couple of students this afternoon.'

A few minutes later, 'Buck', Michael Lund, tapped on my office door and stuck his head in, "Tone, I'm heading home. My last student just cancelled. Things aren't looking too good... Nothing much on the schedule next week either."

"OK, Buck," I responded, "I'll give you a call if something comes up."

No matter how hard we tried over the next few weeks, times had gone bad in Anchorage. Very few students were scheduling flights for training.

I remember one of our pilots saying, "Tony, the way things are going, there's going to be a lot of big boy toys scattered all over the hillsides."

Sure enough, it happened, no one was flying for recreation. It was as if the final curtain had fallen on the good times theater. There were lots of disappointed people at Arctic Basin Airways, including myself. However, there's a time and place for everything and I suppose you might say that Arctic Basin Airways Flying Club was a wonderful happening and hopefully many were left with good memories of those days.

Out of necessity, I, like the other flight instructors, began the task of looking for other work. At least by this time, I had built up my Alaska flight hours and gained some more knowledge and experience.

After a few days of searching, I wandered into Wilbur's; a family owned and operated Charter Company and flight school. My first impression was that they ran a very professional aviation business. The reception area was very large, neat and clean, with all the right stuff around. Terri Mitchell at the counter was very helpful and friendly.

After talking with her and one of the flight instructors for a time, they sent me to meet with Rich Wilbur, the Chief Pilot. I found him to be congenial but very down to business. He liked my resume and made me a job offer by the end of the interview, pending a background check and so on.

Of course, this is just the beginning of getting on line with any company. There's a lot of training and testing required which takes time. However, to begin earning some money, he sent me to their Chief Flight Instructor. After a thorough checkout, I went to work there as a Flight Instructor and soon began working my way up to becoming a Line Pilot with 'Wilbur's, 'The Family Airline'.

This company had grown from a small Flight School through the years, then a Cessna Flight Center, then into one of the largest 135 Businesses in Alaska.

Although most of my time with the company was flying everything from Single Cessnas, Piper Turbo Arrows, Senecas, and Cessna 400 Series aircraft, it was the road to my first Turbo Prop Position!

Things had begun to develop from a Charter Business into flying a mix of more structured Scheduled Runs.

The Company then purchased two Beech 99 Airliners. (Two Pilots and 15 Passenger Configuration).

Several of us quickly graduated into the Aircraft. Wilbur's like many other companies was very good at moving a pilot up the ranks after they had proven themselves. From there most of us continued our careers into flying continuously Turbo Props and Jets, some on to Heavy Jets with Major Airlines.

Here's a story regarding our Beech 99, aVolcanic Eruption, Weather, and Pilot Decision making you, yourself may have to face if you work in Alaska!

Our work there seemed generally to always consider Volcanic Activity.

MT. REDOUBT ERUPTION DECEMBER 1989 -

Mt. Redoubt 1989 **Where's the top of the mountain?**

The Mt. Redoubt eruption of 1989 created severe havoc for aviation. Rich Wilbur, after he had left Wilbur's as Chief Pilot, was the Captain of a Metro Liner with all seats filled and was transitioning across from Illiamna to Anchorage. He was within a few miles of Mt. Redoubt when it blew its top. There was no warning from any source. The volcano was in his 12 o'clock position, right in front of him. He executed a very hard, steep turn and left the area with due haste! No damage was done, but had he been three minutes ahead of schedule, he wouldn't have told me the story.

The eruption went on for days with the dangerous ash cloud flowing with the winds aloft. We'd all been avoiding the ash cloud of course, canceling numerous flights, westbound and south, depending on the winds aloft and the pilot reports of where the cloud was and where it was forecast to be.

This particular evening, I was assigned Captain on Wilbur's Scheduled Flight to McGrath. The aircraft was the B-99 Airliner.

My First Officer and I were both surprised to have an FAA Inspector introduce himself just as we were closing the door.

We had a full aircraft and of course, the inspector got a front row seat right behind us.

Mike quickly adjusted our Weight and Balance and notified the company.

The weather had begun to deteriorate due to a front moving into the Anchorage bowl area.

I had continuously checked weather and didn't really like the trend I was seeing. I had made numerous calls to Flight Service, ATC and other agencies, trying to track the plume of the volcano. The best analysis showed that the plume could be near our route of flight, but they were having trouble tracking it due to the poor weather conditions and precipitation.

We decided to go ahead with the flight at this point however as we had a decent ceiling which would allow us to visually see the ash cloud should it drop into our flight path. We also had radar aboard which possibly would help us spot the ugly monstrous cloud.

We taxied out to runway 6-L and were number three for takeoff, then it started to rain more heavily, indicating an even more unstable condition. I became more uneasy about the situation in that with the increased Precipitation now I felt I could not be sure where the plume was. I turned to the F.O. Mike, "Mike, I'm not going to takeoff."

"What......?"

"I'm not going to takeoff.

"What are you thinking?" he asked.

"Aw, it's the Ash Cloud. With this much weather activity, I don't think we'll be able to get a visual on it, nor a reliable radar reading. It's just too chancy," I explained.

My Rule of Three... Night, Weather Deteriorating, Volcano Plume missing.

"Sounds great to me, but the company's gonna' have a cow what with a Full Boat and all!" he answered.

"I don't care. I just don't feel good about it," I said as I turned to the inspector.

"Inspector Smith, I'm terminating this flight due to the weather. I think the conditions are too unstable and might prevent us from getting a visual on the Ash Cloud."

The FAA Inspector wrote something on his clipboard he'd been using to do his check and said, "Well....., that looks like Good Judgment to me as he completed his notes and slammed his booklet shut. Let's go home!"

He seemed quite relieved that his night was over. I know I was.

We told ground control our intention and got permission to taxi down the runway and to parking after the last Jet took off.

We notified passengers of our situation and intention and received not one negative response. One passenger, "Sounds good to us!"

Back to the gate however, the Inspectors night was not over. As we finished unloading the aircraft, an Epic Story of Heroism began!

Randy, one of our linemen came running out. "Hey Tony, there's a 747 inbound with all four engines out!!!"

As we quickly climbed aboard our aircraft, we picked up on frequency with ATC.

It seems a KLM 747 was still in a Steep Dive from 35,000 feet inbound for the ILS.

It had flown into the Mt. Redoubt Volcanic Plume and had 4 engines 'Flame Out' simultaneously.

They were fully loaded and dumping fuel in a very steep dive!

By the time we could hear anything on the radio they had successfully restarted and had two engines running somewhere around 13,000 Feet.

Now getting vectors to the ILS. The airport was alive with emergency equipment rushing around and heading for the runway.

As far as I know, he had only those two engines running when he intercepted the ILS. We all expected a disaster. This pilot would have to pull off a super-human feat to get a 300,000 pound 747 to and land on, that runway!

Amazingly, we caught his lights breaking through the darkness about three miles out, descending on final approach. With possibly two engines out, night, unable to see out the front of the aircraft (sand blasted windshield), looking out his left side window, he began to side-slip that huge aircraft like a Cessna 172! to a Perfect Landing.

The only follow up I remember reading, was that he said his radar looked a little more intense and that it got very dark, just before he lost all 4 engines almost simultaneously.!

We looked over the aircraft the next day. All four engines were completely destroyed. The leading edges of every part of the aircraft looked like it had been through a bead sanding machine. The windshield was white and opaque. Those folks were very lucky!

Highest Accolades to Captain Karl Van der Elst and also the Complete Crew! A Miracle Save for sure.

One of our Cessna 172's had an encounter with the same ash cloud several days later. It was a partly cloudy day. They were approaching Talkeetna, when suddenly, with no warning, it started raining a sand-like material down on them. The pilot hadn't noticed the snake-like plume drifting overhead. Luckily, they were in a position to land and they did so quickly. The pilot did an excellent job, shutting down his rough engine and side-slipping his aircraft as his windshield became totally opaque. Other than replacing the Windshield and a little Leading Edge Paint, the aircraft was saved.

Prior to these incidents, there were no training manuals I knew of, that included these last two situations. That's why they call Alaska the Last Great Frontier I suppose. Sometimes you have to write your own manuals as you go along with updating your own limits.

You'll find several stories regarding 135 Flights in Alaska in two earlier books pictured below.

If you do not yet have these two books, you might want to click on the pictures below (if in the digital book) and download or order the Print Copies. After that I believe you will have more of what it's like to be a 135 Pilot in Alaska and learn a little more about how to stay alive.

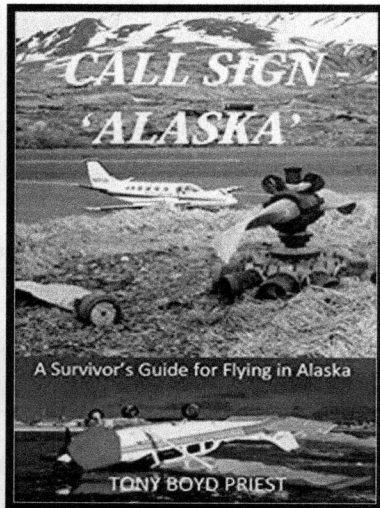

'Call Sign – Iceman' and 'Call Sign – Alaska'
Both are at Amazon.com.

At this point, thought I'd throw in a few more things regarding Alaska Flying.

If you are determined to fly in the Bush, here I would like to add a few general details of how to survive flying into the remote areas into what I call the 'OutBack' – Far from civilization.

Here goes.

For Alaskan Charter Pilots, there's roughly two months of Summer – July and maybe most of August! For Float Planes possibly a little longer.

The reason is of course colder temperatures aloft which can create Icing Conditions.

SURVIVING ALASKA'S CHALLENGES

What type of person flies in Alaska with its great distances, unforgiving terrain and unpredictable weather? All types of course.

If you're one who is looking to have a good long and successful tour here's some characteristics to look for.

He or she...
- Has high stick and rudder skills, technical knowledge of the aircraft, weather, and a high level of instrument skill.
- Is willing to learn from other's experience.
- Knows the aircraft's and his/her personal limitations.
- Has complete reverence for the scope of the challenges that can appear in front of them.

- Has tons of intestinal fortitude that enables them to meet every challenge with control and a clear state of mind.
- Does not take chances or live on bravado with a giant ego that has no boundaries.
- Knows when to use a calculated risk but always leaves an 'out'.
- Is not complacent in tasks or travels. In Alaska,

KNOW THIS....

In Alaska Yesterday Does Not Equal Today! Change Is the Constant!

There's been more than 500 Pilots killed in Alaska. Most were not flying alone. The same incidents and accidents are continuing to occur almost daily!

Always be willing to discuss, read or listen to other's experiences and learn from them so perhaps you can have a long and successful career.

Accident Chains – What is an 'Accident Chain'?

In aviation we refer to it as a series of controllable events or decisions that culminate in an accident.

If you closely analyze most aircraft accidents you can see a chain of events or decisions that lead Pilots on to the accident.

If you recognize a chain of events in progress it's up to you the Pilot in Command to call it at that point. Make a decision to terminate the flight, change a planned route or your destination. Pilot readiness, aircraft condition and limitations of both, the weather, Airport Runway conditions, routing, etc. can all be a part of an Accident Chain.

Watch this carefully especially in Alaska. Some poor decisions might have a survivable outcome in the lower 48, but in Alaska a small bad decision leading to an accident chain can easily become fatal!

Consider this. If an accident is completely avoidable and the wrong decisions are made leading directly to the accident, was it really an unavoidable accident or Pilot error. Several small calculated risks can compound.

'Captain Tony's Rule of Three'

As most know, I stop everything via my 'Rule of Three'. That is, three elements or factors such as a failed instrument, engine problem, deteriorating weather, a questionable Navigation Device, not feeling well whatever added up means Three Strikes. You're Out!

Even if all of three discrepancies occur but are listed within your Master Equipment List which says do this and do that then ok to go. I'm out...

It's the 4ᵗʰ one that gets you.
Time to Taxi back or return to the Airport

It's worked for me so far. It might work for you.

Having worked for several companies in Alaska which included several years of Medevac Missions, I managed to experience just about every aspect of flying Alaska has to offer and visited practically every segment of the Great Land, logged over 10,000 hours Alaska time in everything from Super Cubs to Cessna 206 and 207's to Cessna 310's, 402's to Navajos to a Conquest II. The most exotic aircraft flown was the Helio Courier. Landed on the Numbers once at Merrill Field and turned off still on the Numbers. Amazing Bird.

A lot has changed since the 80's and 90's but I question, with all the technical improvements in aircraft and especially navigation, why hasn't the accident rate improved more? Some reasons of course are the Terrain, the Long Distances, Unpredictable Weather, Risk Management Assessments and Decision Making.

Sometimes those assessments and decisions have to be made in only seconds.

The Accident Chains presented in all **'Call Sign' Books** may reveal a lesson that will help you recognize one of your own controllable links in an ongoing chain.

Break the Chain Now! Live to fly another day.

In a land as vast as Alaska, things happen. Accidents are frequent with many airplanes never found. Many times, it's not because the Pilot was a poor Pilot. He may have been a good Pilot that got into a lot of bad circumstances. We've found through the years that many accidents are simply the last link in a long chain of events such as some of those presented in earlier books.

Alaska has the best Search and Rescue organizations in the world, but just like searching the ocean, you're looking for a needle in a haystack.

Alaska is big. The states of Texas, California, and Montana combined will fit easily within its' borders. It's more than 2,000 miles across, has several mountain ranges and the highest mountain in America, has 3 million lakes, 10,000 streams and rivers and live volcanoes. There's just over a million people living there with most of the population living in Anchorage and Fairbanks.

Alaska attracts adventurous Pilots by the hundreds. Employers sometime hire low time Pilots just because they need Pilots. The way I look at it though, Alaska is not a good place to build time, and Florida is not good training ground for Alaska flying. Reno yes. Florida or Kansas no.

If you decide to take on your own Alaskan Adventure, whether as a Pilot, traveler, adventurer, mountain climber, or to work there keep in mind that Alaska, the Yukon Territory, and N.W. British Columbia are all very much wilderness.

PHYSICAL FITNESS

Like most of Alaska there's deep wilderness beauty everywhere leaving you in awe with the ever-changing scenery.

It's easy to just climb into your aircraft and where occasionally your flight is like sitting on your sofa at home, taking in the amazing beauty of this State.

In general, one of the most important things you should do however is to

<u>Get in Shape and Stay in Shape</u>.

Alaska commercial flying can be physically strenuous in several aspects.

Just getting though turbulence, or encountering a minus 50-degree weather event, or high winds while on glare ice, loading a stretcher or handling heavy cargo all after sitting enroute for 3+ hours. You get what I mean.

Being in shape is extremely important should you have to survive on your own after a bad engine or mishap.

Again, an incident in the Lower 48 may cause an inconvenience. The same incident in Alaska may become fatal!

New meaning is applied to the phrase "Be Prepared"

Keep the 'What Ifs' in mind always.

Be Very Wary of some of the U Tube Videos posted of Weekenders presenting themselves as experienced and doing incredibly Dumb Things!

Make sure all your Stick and Rudder Skills are sharp!

Bush Flying Last Word...

Remember, once you leave Anchorage or Fairbanks, you're suddenly very low on the Food Chain.

You might want to Target Practice with a 12 Gauge Pump. Carry with it both Bird Shot and Buck Shot along with a Glock 20 or something comparable.

Birdshot of course for food. A couple of Buckshot Rounds to the Shoulder of a Grizz to break him down, then go for the Kill. Both are Powerful Survival Weapons (Lots of Fire Power).

(There was an incident where several hunters with high power rifles were killed one by one after they all had unloaded on the Bear.)

The Glock 20 has twice the ammunition capacity as some and can hit significantly harder.

Look up Alaska Survival Equipment required for aircraft. and Always be ready to Survive.

MUD FLATS...

Although I've landed there a few times for digging Clams, I don't recommend trying it unless you know the area very well and you have a current Tidal Chart. Go for the lowest tide and expect a small window of time.

The mud consistency can change in minutes! And turn into quicksand. Don't want to lose you, your passengers or your airplane! That 30 Foot Bore Tide has killed several folks stuck in the mud!

We're departing the Anchorage area over the Cook Inlet Mudflats at Low Tide.

If you're looking to land off airport anywhere, be sure to go with someone first who is current with those particular areas and very capable. Don't go with just an adventurous Pilot who's only watched those type landings on U Tube.

Be ready to survive on your own. Have a reliable weapon aboard. (You cannot carry Bear Spray in your aircraft Cabin!) Possibly in your Nose Baggage or Wing Locker only.

SOME OF THE ALASKAN MISSIONS THROUGH THE YEARS –

The following are just some of the memorable missions during my 11 years there. As you will see, what a TRIPPP! (Not necessarily in historical order.)

Scientific Studies around Active Volcanic Eruptions with Special Equipment and Modified Aircraft – Mt. Saint Augustine 1986 / Mt. Redoubt 1989 (Alaska)

Serviced many Villages bringing in Groceries, Medical supplies, Equipment, Parts, etc. for some really great Folks.

Of course, Hunters and Fishermen to some very interesting destinations – tons of short airstrips and landing areas.

Hauled fish (+/-2000 lbs. at a time with minimum fuel of course) from various villages into Anchorage for processing.

Transported Pipeline Workers, Equipment and Tools, landing on Roads and Highways adjacent to the Pipeline.

Organized and Flew Relief for Earthquake / Flood Victims / Fires and the **Prince William Oil Spill**.

Our relief effort for the Oil Spill was primarily focused on Valdez, Cordova and especially the Village of Tatitlek Victims and was organized by Roland Suter (taking the picture), Implemented Corporately by Bill Kelly, Colorado (left) and Gary Kompkoff (Right) Chief of Tatitlek Village, Alaska,. I'm the pilot looking guy in the middle.

USFS Fire Fighting Reconnaissance/Air Attack and flew Smoke Jumpers to various wildfires.

Delivered Entertainers to various Remote Towns.

Transported Parts and Equipment for Aircraft Maintenance to various destinations in Alaska and the Yukon Territory, CA

Med-Evac Missions - Later on, Moved on up somewhat Thanks to a great Friend and Co-Captain Tom Miville. As Chief Pilot, I interviewed and hired Tom at Wilbur's sometime back where he performed very well and did an excellent job.

Down the road about a year, he left for a Conquest II job flying for **Providence Hospital** in Anchorage.

Being the Comrade and Friend he was, he called one day and mentioned they may have a position open. Might want to check.

I did and eventually gave notice to Wilbur's as well. Shortly, found myself headed to Flight Safety in Wichita.

Life Guard Alaska Flight Nurses and Crew Members

Well after 3 years I had built some great Turbo-Prop Time. Saved a lot of Lives of Course, accomplished more than 300 Medevac Missions and was privileged to have experienced practically every nook and cranny of Alaska.

Later, following the Contract expiration with Providence Hospital I began working with **Security Aviation**. (Believe me, once you have years of experience in Alaska, jobs can be plentiful.

With Security, I flew some great missions.

Some Most Memorable –

Bruce Babbitt - Secretary of the Interior on his Alaska Environmental Study Tour - Single Pilot, Full Boat, with News Reporters and Security Personnel, Conquest II.

Walter Hickel - Governor of Alaska, one of our best Clients. (We had to have the right engine turning exactly at the minute he had scheduled. He never missed setting foot on the airstair door at his departure time!)

Flew FAA and performed Flight Tests for N.T.S.B. during accident investigations.

Several Missions with FBI, CIA, FAA, NTSB and Law Enforcement as we were their Preferred Carrier.

Transported State Troopers along with Prisoners on occasion.

Transported Iditarod Dog Sled Teams around.

Flew High Ranking Military Personnel to various Bases and Remote Radar sites.

Of course, I've only skimmed the surface regarding Alaska Aviation.

There is a downside involved as I lost 15 Friends and acquaintances during my 11 years there working in all season's year round.

Most were good Pilots who got into bad circumstances. Following some of their stories, however, an Accident Chain was quite obviously in play.

Some of those stories are set in detail in Call Sign 'Alaska' and other Alaskan Books.

It's important that you absorb all you can from Books to long time Pilots in Alaska to keep an edge of safety. That also goes for just about flying in any wilderness areas.

SOME OF THE AIRCRAFT FLOWN IN ALASKA...

Seems like every Cessna known to man! Includes C152, C172, C170, C180, C185, C195, C206, C207, C210, C310, C336, C337, C402, C404, and C441.

As I worked for a Piper Dealer for a time, pretty much covered all the Piper Singles with tons of time in the Turbo Arrow. Quite a lot of time in Navajos.

Accumulated 300 + hours in miscellaneous Tail Draggers, Cessna 170B, Taylor Craft, Luscombe, J-3 Cub, Citabria, Super Cubs (Occasionally with Tundra Tires), and the H 295 Helio Courier and others.

H-295, an amazing aircraft to fly!

The H-295 Helio Courier has plenty of power and is a great STOL Aircraft. With Spring Loaded Slats, Take Offs and Landings can be very short. Slow Flight is Awesome. It's a surprise when the Slats Pop Out the first time. On Takeoff, a little uncomfortable to rotate at 30 Knots.

~

Well, Life Changes sometimes occur. I had Family both in California and Georgia so thought I'd solve the traveling problem and head to the middle of the Country.

Denver seemed like the most likely place to go.

As a current 135 Pilot, getting a Flying Position is usually not a problem. I was looking forward to living in one of the most Recreational States.

However – Alaska was Certainly an Experience of a Lifetime!

Looking back on my long career I've come to the conclusion that ...

Out of all the Accomplishments and Flying I've ever done, Alaska was and is the most Memorable, Gratifying, Soul Fulfilling Flying I've ever had!

CHAPTER 7

COLORADO BASE

New to the area, I found a couple of situations but settled for a time at Mile High Aviation, a local Flight School at the Jeff Co Airport. (Always keep your CFI Current.) Not long after, working with the Owner, Paul Dickson, a great Pilot and Flight Instructor, we soon had a Part 135 up and running.

With that in place we continued to build a dynamic operation flying all over the Southwest utilizing a Cessna 182RG, C207 and other singles plus one Cessna 402B.

After a couple of years however, I was approached on the Ramp by Rich Bjelkevig of Mountain Aviation, a relatively new 135 Operator on the field.

He introduced himself, "Tony, understand you have 135 experience in a Conquest II?" One thing to another, eventually I gave notice at Mile High and signed up with them.

Times at Mile High Aviation had been great, made a ton of great friends, but here again was a great 135 opportunity to fly Turbo Props. (Thank you, Captain Bill Arnott, **"Aim and Climb Higher."**)

Wasn't long after, I was once again at Flight Safety and soon flying the Conquest traveling all over the country.

I had been specifically assigned that aircraft for about six months, then returning from a week of personal vacation back in Georgia, as I walked in the door, "Tony, the Conquest is no longer! It has been T Boned by a sleepy lineman on a tug, hit Broadside. Your aircraft was totaled!"

My first thought was 'What now.'

However, a few days later, I was still on Mountain Aviation payroll, in another Sim School down in Texas, checking out in their newly acquired B200 Super King Air, then back in Colorado, their BE90, then eventually flying several versions of the 90 and once again flying all over Colorado, the West and the U.S.

That was some really great flying, continuing to build Turbo-Prop time.

In case you are headed to Colorado, here's a review of some Basics along with some various experiences you may be interested in.

Just a note, Colorado has a lot of higher elevation Airports than Alaska! Alaska's more Pass Flying whereas in this case you're dealing with somewhat different circumstances.

One of the most mountainous states, VFR it's easy to navigate the Front Range. From Denver headed north keep the mountains to your left. Headed South keep the mountains to your right! Guess that's where easy ends.

Mountain Ranges here are generally aligned North and South. Winds are prevailing westerlies, a perfect setup for Orographic enhanced Thunderstorms.

If possible, you might plan the majority of your flying in the morning hours to avoid Turbulence.

In Summer, Density Altitude is a Major Factor. High Humidity or fog from a passing Thunderstorm further enhances the problem.

For example, here's a common error and incident checking out a new Pilot in our Cessna 172 to high terrain flying. He was from out of town, had just over a hundred hours but no mountain experience.

One of the items we discussed was Normal Aspirated Engine Performance generally above +/- 4,000 feet.

Following a normal runup and mag check, prior to departure, we did a full static runup while leaning the mixture to peak RPM then enrich slightly for best takeoff power.

After discussion of other hazards involved in everyday flights, we departed the runway at Jeffco Airport, BJC (now Rocky Mountain Metropolitan Airport, Elevation 5,673 ft.). Density Altitude was about 8,000 feet that day. Not unusual in summer months.

On our initial climb he continued to raise the nose due to his low climb rate. I reminded him to watch his airspeed and not to slow any further due to possibly getting into a stall condition.

As we approached the departure end of the runway, he once again raised the nose, this time with a full stall warning indication. I said "My aircraft!", lowered the nose slightly, accelerated and recovered to level flight at about 200 feet. As we continued to accelerate, I began a slow climb at 300 feet per minute.

During our air work in the practice area, we further discussed Density Altitude and its effect on takeoffs as well as landings.

After completing our flight and more discussion, he expressed his doubts about flying in these conditions and decided not to continue.

On the flip side of summer, the winter months here are very spectacular and inviting to enter. However, be aware that weather can change dramatically in a very short period. Icing, turbulence, up and down drafts, and mountain wave conditions are common occurrences.

If you are lucky enough to fly up to take a day of skiing, depending on temperatures, before departure, ensure your aircraft engine is thoroughly warmed as well as your cabin.

Cabin?... I've mentioned this in the past that windshields and sometimes instruments can have condensation from the heater moisture and frost over in a cold cockpit!

If you're flying in from Kansas in May, remember, some Colorado mountain destinations may still be running below freezing at night. Are you running 100 Wt. oil? Might consider a multi-grade or lighter weight as required. Always good to check with a local Mechanic.

Last thing, as in Alaska or flying in any mountainous terrain, always be sure you have the appropriate survival gear aboard for the season. Even in Summer, it can get very cold up there.

Ceiling, if possible, 2,000 feet above your highest routing terrain – Visibility 15 miles.

Mountain top winds in a Colorado Winter commonly are 30 + knots where you can expect moderate turbulence.

Generally, stay 10% below Gross Weight at least. Use those Performance Charts! Drop your numbers down another 10% to be on the green side.

I've done night and IFR operations in the Rockies but usually in Turbine Aircraft. Not recommended for light general aviation aircraft.

Make sure you have the magnetic course for each leg of the flight. Monitor the heading being flown so as not to enter the wrong valley leading to high terrain or a possible dead end.

Pay strict attention to your Performance charts. Climb back and forth until well clear of the highest crossing terrain plus 1500 – 2000 feet at least 3 miles before reaching your crossing point or the highest elevation required in the pass.

RAPID WEATHER CHANGES

To give you an idea of how fast weather can change especially around Denver... Stopped into Taco Bell for lunch.

It was 62 degrees. About the time I finished lunch, it was snowing, not just flurries, Snowing Heavy!

Another time I'd been on a two-day charter and upon my late-night arrival back at Jeffco, found my car covered in ice! No not just light ice, the entire car was covered from top to bottom with wheels totally frozen to the ground. A literal block of ice.

Had to get a ride home and the next day the line crew drug my car into a hangar for thawing. Took another day!

Might be time for an Alternate Route!

When you're deep in the mountains, this rapidly changing weather can become a very serious threat.

An Alternate Route comes in handy when an unforeseen weather event begins blocking your first route. If simply transitioning, might look at IFR, 'I Follow Road' as there's a couple of Freeways running through the Rockies. Even so, not only is there a chance of your visibility dropping, there are obstacles. Tunnels may transition the road below mountains that will require you to go up and around the mountain. Scrutinize your route very carefully, IFR or I.F.R.!

Really scrutinize the entire weather pattern before your departure. If you glance toward the mountains and see a Standing Lenticular Cloud, might want to rethink your mission for the day.

Having supplemental oxygen aboard is not a bad thing either... just in case you have to escape some weather and cross higher terrain. If you have a non-turbo aircraft, you're probably close to being maxed out in most of these passes.

Don't expect IFR pop up clearances, especially during busy Skiing months. Plan well ahead and expect weather to be a factor. If VFR, File a Flight Plan and show your exact planned route.

As I continually suggest, keep a Sectional on your lap, have your Prominent Terrain Features identified as well as your Escape Routes. The reason why – Magnetic Disturbance Areas, a phenomenon you might encounter which I have flying in these magnificent mountains. There will be on occasion variations on your magnetic compass headings! Mark the correct side of the peak or ridgeline on your route.

I've only touched on some of the hazards as there's many, and remember it's up to you the Pilot to make the right decisions in flight planning, preparation and dealing with whatever Mother Nature throws your way!

'ACCIDENT CHAIN' -

There's plenty of opportunities to start up an Accident Chain. If you closely analyze most Colorado aircraft accidents you can see a chain developed along the way.

If you recognize a chain of events in progress it's up to you, the Pilot in Command to call it at that point, decide to terminate the flight or change a planned route of flight or destination. Pilot and or aircraft readiness and limitations, the weather, airport and runway conditions, routing, etc. can all be a part of an accident chain. Remember - 'Captain Tony's Rule of Three'.

Three Links recognized – Make another plan!

BAGGAGE DOOR -

Why die over a stupid baggage door!!!

It happens folks.

Again, an incident turned into an accident at Jeffco Airport.

A 201J Mooney departed on a high D.A. day. On takeoff he had a baggage door pop open, called the Tower and intended to return for a landing.

Evidently distracted from his primary job – **Fly the Stupid Airplane** - Stalled and killed two! Absolutely no call for this accident and loss of life.

Two Baggage Door incidents in Alaska took 13 Lives! Why?!!! Both over water, a fully loaded Navajo and a fully loaded Caravan!

It doesn't matter where you are.

If you're flying a Brick... Fly the Brick! To a landing! Maintain Airspeed! <u>Do Not Stall!</u> Land or Crash land in a controlled manner at least whether on water or on land!

Cessna Grand Caravan on Ramp at BJC

Had the privilege to fly this magnificent aircraft!
On one occasion landed and took off from the old Bull Frog,
Utah runway. 9 folks with baggage. Only took ½ of the 3,000
Ft. Runway!

Day to Day – Leave some Margins –
Break out the charts.

One thing's for sure... Every Pilot needs to know his
aircraft and personal limitations. After they're set, have the
discipline and courage to stand by them! Be prepared to walk
away from any job if pressed to go beyond those limitations.

As Pilot in Command, as mentioned numerous times, don't
be persuaded to do something you are not comfortable with.
If you Err'..., Err'... on the Green Side, Not the RED! Fly a long
time.

FIREFIGHTING – AIR ATTACK!

Our company attained authorization with several Federal Agencies including U.S. Forest Service. Reconnaissance/Air Attack/Personnel Transportation (California, Colorado, and New Mexico.)

Every summer, we were alert for Thunderstorms with associated Lightning Strikes.

Forestry had a trailer adjacent to their Dirt Airstrip where on occasion we would spend our days.

We primarily utilized our Cessna 182RG (Retractable) to run Forestry Agents from one smoke area to another.

Our primary duty was to spot fires, fly around them, observe fuel available for the fires, wind direction, etc.

The Agent aboard made judgement calls regarding anything appearing hazardous to people, structures, whether to call in a Tanker or Smoke Jumpers.

The process – We looked for smoke areas generally following Thunderstorms, then go from one to the other, discover the most threatening.

For instance, on my first day on duty, one fire we found burning extremely strong was burning upslope toward the top of a mountain about 30 miles from Denver. I was surprised when after circling this large windblown fire, the Agent took a look around and said, 'not a problem, let's go to the next one.

He then explained that although it was a heck of a fire, had no potential to harm a population or damage property. Our first duty was to population and structures.

Not sure how he categorized it on his report, but we found another shortly after that was a threat. He quickly forwarded the GPS Coordinates.

The process continued through Dispatch that directed the Tankers to those coordinates.

All went well that day.

It was a few days later following another Thunderstorm situation we were dispatched back into the Rockies.

Well that day, we were quite proficient in locating a couple of potentially serious fires.

The first went fine, the second... We'd just forwarded the coordinates, turned to depart and a Tanker Aircraft almost ate our lunch! Guess that's why they call it Air Attack!

We decided to give a little more distance from the actual fire before calling anything in!

Good to know in Colorado they have a very serious Fire Fighting process and a well-tuned Forestry Department.

Not sure if other states have the same system as their 'Johnny on the Spot' Procedures.

"MILITARY'S PLAYING GAMES."

I'd just departed Sidney, Nebraska VFR cleared to intercept my IFR GPS Course to Denver when I noted my headings were not correct. I'd been on this route many times and knew the mountains and terrain well. My GPS swore Denver was 300 degrees!

'I know where Denver is!' I thought to myself as I gained altitude. I disregarded my GPS as I had a visual on the Rocky Mountain Range and made my turn to intercept the airway.

Shortly I was able reach Center and reported on a visual departure, looking for a vector direct Denver.

Center complied and left me about on the same heading I was flying.

I mentioned my GPS was indicating Denver as Northwest instead of Southwest!

He came back. "Yep. Just came up. Military's playing games. They've moved Denver! Disregard your GPS. Remain on the Airway for now."

"Roger that!" Never heard of anything like that. I'd just gained a little more respect for Backups.

The Military can do anything they want without warning in case of an emergency. Guess they have to test the systems occasionally.

Always have Navigational Backups working right along with your GPS System. Crosscheck Instruments and watch for discrepancies!

Later on I had another episode flying over the Florida Pan Handle enroute to Tampa, Florida, FL 250 in our Citation Mustang.

Center called, "Military's taking control of GPS. Disregard and Expect Radar Vectors for the next 100 miles."

Then in about 5 minutes he had me on an Airway. So, that can happen folks!

Just a note about GPS and I Pads... Everybody's flying with them. Great technology of course. However, keep other Nav Backups going.

I've personally had 4 incidents where they've gone blank. One at a critical time descending into a very busy airport area. Luckily, I had backups tuned in and was able to continue. At least two of the failures were heat related from sunlight through the windshield.

(Although I use GPS like everyone else, even in my car, I carry a Chart or Map. Most don't realize that if the U.S. comes under attack the Military can Close any Freeway needed. Most debunk the theory but I believe there are specific little-known Freeway stretches designated for off airport Military landings! Also, if GPS fails or Interstate closed for any reason, nice to have a map aboard.)

CONTROLLER ERROR? –

Denver International Airport –

Here's a unique experience on a blue-sky early morning, I followed 5 miles in trail of Air Force One.

Compared to his roll out, mine was later and of course much shorter.

Air Force One and I were both cleared "Taxi to parking." while on the same Taxiway but basically at two different ends of the runway.

Rolling along, I observed the Big Blue 747 continuing to come my way.

I checked in with Ground, mentioned, "Should I hold short of Taxiway Echo?" ... Pause.............

"Conquest 46BC, Hold short of Echo."

I did and gave him plenty of room, "Roger Hold Short of Echo, 6BC."

"Air Force One, The Conquest is holding short of Echo."

"Roger, Air Force One."

Nose to Nose with Air Force One!

"46BC, Taxi to Parking Follow the 747."

He parked at a remote corner of the Ramp area. I was marshalled close to the FBO.

(Always know where you are and be responsible for your own situational awareness, even on the ground, at large airports especially with 15 controllers watching / not watching. - Just sayin')

~

Well, I'd spent about 5 years in Colorado, some really great flights, great aircraft and made lot's of friends.

Regretfully I had to say goodbye. Again.

With my aging Mom needing more help back home, we decided to move on back to Georgia.

What a great experience and privilege to fly in Colorado, the Rocky Mountains and points North, South, East and West! Great People, Unbelievable Vistas, really great Skiing. Sure, miss all that.

'Flying the Rockies' has many Challenges but really worth the effort if you get a chance to work there.

Always remember to Leave yourself an Out!
Totally Respect Density Altitude, yes, at <u>all</u> Destinations!

CHAPTER 8

BACK TO GEORGIA

Once again flying Medevacs now with Georgia Jet and Critical Care Med-Flight, primarily utilizing King Air 200's. I found myself all up and down the East Coast in all types of weather. It was pretty good duty of course, had several great Co-Pilots and really enjoyed working with the Medical Folks again.

However, about a year down the road, one of my Charter Customers approached me and asked if he purchased a King Air, would I be interested in coming to work for him. 'You Bet'cha I did.'

A few weeks later, I received a call, gave my two weeks' notice and found myself back at Flight Safety in Wichita and Flying a new Super King Air B200 with 230 hours Total Time and with latest Avionics!... On an extremely good salary of course. 'Cloud 9.'

TELLURIDE AND COMPANY – BACK TO COLORADO ROCKIES!

Now back to Corporate Flying, Our First Flight from Atlanta was to Telluride, Colorado (TEX, Elevation 9,070 feet, Runway Length 7,111 Feet).

('Just came from there.' Life of a Pilot) Probably one of the reasons the company wanted me aboard. I'd flown Charters to Georgia from Denver as well.

It was a great flight out with one stop. From there nonstop into Telluride.

Lots of chatter as everyone was totally enjoying our smooth flight through the Rockies.

As we approached, I gave a before landing brief over the intercom.

Our descent was smooth and very scenic.

However as we turned onto our final approach, the chatter suddenly stopped.

I asked my new first day on the job 'Co-Pilot', my Wife Judy (Her last day at Air Tran was the day before!) to glance back. She did, smiled at our passengers with Thumbs up and to me, "It appears everyone is looking at us."

I thought, 'No... it was the interesting view of the Runway sitting atop a mesa with a cliff on the approach end and a mountain on the other'.

All were courageously looking at the scene but quite silent.

Our approach and landing went smoothly and unbelievably well. We taxied in and all aboard were relieved and jubilant. (This was a First for them.) We all had an awesome First Class Holiday.

Prior to our departure day, after carefully scrutinizing the numbers, I informed the owner we have to be rolling out by 0930 due to Density Altitude.

"Density What?"

"Well, the forecast tomorrow is for higher temperatures with rapid warming in the morning hours. The temperatures forecast will greatly decrease our performance, yes, even on a new King Air 200."

He was good about that and said he would always respect my judgement and assured me all would be there on time.

We were ready at 0900 and soon folks started arriving. A couple of the young children were in pajamas and one lady was brushing her hair, but soon all were aboard, door closed and ready for Taxi at 0935.

Earlier in the morning, I had observed a Lear Jet crew preparing for departure. Heard a 'Top Off' order. So thought to myself, 'they're going out on a Deadhead flight back to home base'.

Well, guess what, about the same time as our first passengers were boarding, six folks arrived in a large van with all their baggage and proceeded to the Lear. They loaded up to what I would guess as Gross Weight. I was amazed as well as concerned.

We were all aboard the King Air with engines running. The Lear had engines running as well. I signaled for them to go ahead. They taxied out as # 1. We followed as # 2.

He did a short check I suppose as they were taxiing, checked in with ATC, Cleared and proceeded to do a rolling takeoff.

I continued to hold short now # 1 for takeoff.

As we watched, their Takeoff was a little unsettling to me. I can imagine what the crew and passengers were thinking.

They used about 7,000 feet of the 7,111-foot runway, then went off the cliff, disappearing down into the canyon.

Thinking the worst, I was amazed when they reappeared a good minute later traveling very low, slowly climbing out of the bottom of the canyon. That was very close! Could have been a fireball in the canyon.

The Captain probably announced 'Giving you a nice scenic tour of the canyon today'. However, I doubt it. I can imagine the tense cockpit and conversation thereafter!

Thus, best to go partial fuel out of there, stop in Denver or Grand Junction, top off then go home.

Our Takeoff went very smoothly and we actually left the runway climbing.

USE THOSE PERFORMANCE CHARTS!
ERR' ON THE GREEN SIDE!

Other than continuous trips west, occasionally we visited several destinations up and down the Eastern U.S.

On occasion we were in the Caribbean visiting Bahamas and other points south.

Some notes to consider:

Although primarily you're close to sea level most of the time, be aware that most of the Islands were created by and are volcanic mountains.) Note: It was very interesting to spend time with totally different cultures through the years. However, in those areas there are a lot of differences.

In the Dominican, leaving the East Coast for the West etc., everyone, including ATC may be speaking Spanish. On one occasion it took 5 Radio Calls before they recognized an 'English' and stopped the Spanish Chatter. After that, everyone began speaking English! Also know that Radar and Communications may be very sparse in some areas.

On Nevis Island, I had to climb a 20 Ft. Ladder to get to their 'Tower' to file a Flight Plan. Guess what, Nobody Home. Figured it all out though. At least the Goats remained on the ground and Monkeys in the trees. (We loved the Island and Accommodations at the Nisbet Plantation.) this was 2002 and I'm sure the airport has improved.

DREAM JOB –

Quite a surprise... "Tony, I want to buy a single engine aircraft to travel occasionally and eventually get my Pilot's license."

"That's awesome Ben."

First thing I knew we had a brand-new Trinidad on the line.

Well, we did train on occasion, eventually took some short trips. Then this surprise...

Ben, "I would like to do some Island hopping in the Bahamas for a few days. Sound okay? We can bring the Wives."

'Have to think about that one. NOT......'

"Absolutely Ben. Love to do that trip."

"Let's depart Monday morning. Can you get us ready by then?"

"Sure can."

Well, his idea was to Island Hop literally two or three islands daily. However, our Ladies were now involved.

Turned out when I got the final itinerary, we had a 21-day trip with 2 or 3 overnights at every destination.

Some of the Islands included were Nassau, Turks and Caicos, Nevis Island in the West Indies, Puerto Rico, St. Thomas, and a Resort on the west coast of the Dominican Republic. Wow... A Dream no one has ever had.

Back on topic, concerning these flights, as mentioned, most are mountainous destinations! Yep.

Generally, IFR is ok however, communication and radar coverage were not that great. You had to know where you were at all times with few reliable navaids which took some planning.

The Dominican is very mountainous and with weather and poor communications can be a challenge.

Nevis Island basically is a Volcano with a large Cone at the end of the runway 10. Plenty of turbulence, plan a quick turn around the cone and adjust onto a short final and you'll typically land in crosswinds coming off the mountain.

BERMUDA TRIANGLE -

On one such outing, we were headed to Nassau and experienced the infamous Instrument Failure in the Triangle.

We're cruising along at about 15,000 feet, clear beautiful VFR Day.

Suddenly, I noticed my magnetic compass begin to move around. Then all my gyros were spinning around.

"What the..."

I'd heard about these events happening out here, but... This was really strange. A new aircraft, latest instruments... Spinning? Good thing we were visual.

After about 2 minutes, all the gyros slowed and finally stopped spinning. My magnetic compass settled.

Guess that confirms other reports I'd heard.

Since then, traveling many times in the area, I've had no other anomalies.

TUESDAY, SEPTEMBER 11, 2001 -

It was a beautiful clear day for flying. My 'Co-Pilot' for our King Air 200 was Judy, my Wife.

Our Company officers including the Company President had shown up early and were ready to go.

All went well with ATC and soon we were at FL 250, 25,000 Feet.

Ben, the President suddenly appeared in the cockpit with his cell phone.

"Tony, I just got a call that said one of the Twin Towers had been hit by an aircraft.

At that time, we thought it might be an accident.

Shortly after, he came forward again and said

"Another plane has hit the second Tower! We could be under a Terrorist attack!"

"Sure, sounds like it, "I was about to key the mike.

ATC called, "Attention all aircraft on this frequency. The United States is under a Terrorist Attack. Every aircraft on this frequency plan to proceed to the nearest suitable airport for landing!"

Now constant ATC – Airline Chatter. Delta, United, American and others.

I asked Judy to pull out our local VFR Chart to check airports in the vicinity as we were about to be handed off to the next controller.

ATC, "Charlotte Airspace is now closed to all traffic."

ATC, "N45BC (Our Aircraft) you're about to enter Charlotte Airspace. What are your intentions?"

By this time, we'd identified a VFR Destination prospect, Rock Hill, South Carolina about 50 miles west.

"Center, N45BC, if you can clear us below 18,000, we can proceed VFR direct to Uniform Zulu Alpha, Rock Hill, South Carolina."

"Roger, 45BC, Turn left Heading 270 degrees, cleared to 18,000. Expedite descent, call 18,000, then plan to proceed VFR direct Uniform Zulu Alpha."

Well, I began unwinding my altitude at 4,000 feet per minute on our assigned heading.

Shortly, "Center, 45BC passing 18,000 proceeding direct to Rock Hill, Cancel IFR."

"Roger 45BC Good Luck!"

"Thanks, 45BC"

By this time Center had become extremely busy working with Airliners all over the place.

ATC - Center, "ALL AIRCRAFT STAND BY!".

"ATTENTION, every aircraft that can hear my voice, "ON THE GROUND NOW!!! The Military is taking charge of airspace and F-16s have been scrambled."

We were already complying and descending like the space shuttle.

Judy had contacted Rock Hill and received landing information.

I asked her to keep an eye on our Traffic Alert System to see if any targets appeared anywhere, especially behind us!

I'd continued our free fall descent and now was at tree top level at max speed.

There was no other traffic at the airport so I made a straight in approach and landed.

Ben came forward and said they were talking with the Airport and were getting rental cars to drive home and suggested we do the same.

As soon as we passed out the luggage, everyone disappeared. We went about our normal duties securing the aircraft.

Since not knowing how long this emergency would be going, we decided to stay with the aircraft. Hopefully we could fly home in two or three days.

We proceeded to a hotel and watched the news and live coverage of the horrific events still unfolding.

We ended up staying 3 days, then realized no one would be able to fly for another week.

Back to a rental car search. None... However, we finally found an old van to rent and headed home. What a horrific time. Horrific news and images.

After being home for a few days, we finally received a Slot Assignment to bring our aircraft back to Atlanta.

We again in the old van, braved the mountain roads and arrived back at Rock Hill.

Our flight home went well. Just weird as we were the only aircraft in the sky in Atlanta Airspace! There was no ATC chatter, all was silent except for our one controller. The Blue Skies were totally empty.

~

Primarily our continuing destinations were business trips, with occasional flights to attend Golf Tournaments, College Football Games, Race Car events and to Colorado, a favorite destination.

One memorable trip to Rifle for an Elk hunt, we had to standby for 6 days! Bummer... Not quite. Judy and I were blessed to be able to tour and enjoy several locations in the Rockies.

We traveled back and forth almost every week to Dallas, Phoenix, Denver, El Paso, and occasionally Los Angeles for Business Meetings.

The King Air was comfortable, quiet, a beautiful Corporate Aircraft in practically every way. However,

One day on our return from Dallas, as we approached an impassible line of Super Cells I had to begin deviating to the north.

Change, the Constant in General Aviation.

I advised the passengers of this and was surprised when Ben came forward. As he surveyed the incredible wall ahead, "Tony, if we had a Jet could we fly over this line of storms?"

"Well Ben, there are several Jets that can easily get over the top of these. As you can see, we're about maxed out in this aircraft."

"OK, I plan to look into it when we get home."

A couple of weeks later, "Tony, think you can fly a B400A, Beech Jet?"

"Certainly, do Ben... Will have to schedule a Sim School of course."

"Not a problem," he said thoughtfully.

A few weeks later we had sold our BE200 King Air and had on the ramp a beautiful B400A!

Off to pretty challenging School of course. By this time I'd managed to attain some Citation I and II time which helped somewhat however the B400A is a completely different machine.

A tough Sim Course for sure but came out as a Captain.

Afterwards I needed to accomplish my 25 hours I.O.E. before flying our aircraft as Captain and so we brought on another BE400 Captain until I had that time. Did that and there we were. Our Flight Department was really on the move literally.

Our 45,000 feet took care of most Thunderstorms!

The schedules and duties were really outstanding. The aircraft was really fast! The Owner was great to fly for.

Some notes for flying the Beech Jet 400A. -

It's <u>Fast</u>. With Noise Abatement Areas measuring Decibels and Low Initial Clearance Altitudes along with Speed Limitations it can be a little uncomfortable at times. Pulling back power as soon as the gear hits the wells doesn't seem natural.

What? No Ailerons? Spoilers only... If you're used to using Side Slips in crosswinds forget it. Takes a little time to get used to but after a few flights seems to work out ok. Be Cautious on your numbers and the impulse to side slip at slow speed.

On ours, we had an occasional Thrust Reverser that wouldn't engage. Watch that of course on your roll out. Maintenance could not identify any kind of problem.

What we found was to 'plant' the aircraft a little more solidly on the asphalt. Seemed to take care of the problem.

On one landing in the rain, I accidently 'greased it on' where as the owner came forward and jokingly asked "What happened on that landing?" The TRs worked fine that day.

<u>Fuel</u> can get cold even with the heating system. FL450 can generally be 65 – 69 below zero.

We watched the Fuel Temp Gauge when at high altitude and began our descent well before Redline (usually +/- 100 NM from our destination). Always like to keep some power throughout. (There were at least two incidents reported where flameouts occurred at Flight Level.)

Get lower as soon as possible for arrival at your destination. The Aircraft is built for speed, not pattern work.

Once getting used to those anomalies we enjoyed flying the aircraft immensely. Passengers loved it.]

However, Maintenance costs were pretty high and after a year or so of operations, the company decided to put the aircraft on a 135 Certificate to help with the cost.

We did. Took our FAA Check Rides and with the new business, hired two new Co-Pilots.

With this aircraft and Part 135, we flew throughout the U.S. (Logged time was slow to build simply because the aircraft was so darn fast!) We generally flew direct, higher and faster than most airlines.

After another great year of flying, and as Corporate Dream Jobs can go, one day as Chief Pilot I'm sitting with the President and Chief Financial Officer going over Financial Spreadsheets.

We took some actions to cut back through different avenues, but then another meeting the next Quarter...

Needless to say, several of us were looking for work shortly thereafter.

BACK TO FLIGHT INSTRUCTING FOR A WHILE.

As mentioned earlier, keep that CFI License Current for possible gaps along the way.

Living one of our dreams, in our beautiful Home on West Point Lake, LaGrange, GA, after looking around a bit for another 135 Job, I settled for a time with the local Flight School.

Jacob Luigens, a really great Pilot, Instructor, Mechanic and Friend, owned Air Ventures, a really dynamic flight school with several aircraft. (I'd instructed in all the aircraft in the past.)

He graciously brought me aboard as Chief Flight Instructor. There, I was training students in Warriors, Diamonds and Multi in a Piper Seneca. We licensed several Pilots through the period.

During that time I'd become fairly close friends with Peter Van Leewan, a good Friend and great mechanic from Boston. He was the 'Go To' man for just about any major maintenance problem.

Down the road he asked me one day if I would have any interest in flying one of the owners of a C421B up to North Carolina.

135

I had time in the 421 and soon met up with David Sandlin, one of the owners, a retired Air Force Officer.

After a thorough check out in the aircraft, soon I was flying Part 91 with their Company.

I was back cross country flying throughout the mountains of North Carolina, in winter, flying their Cessna 421.

After finishing up a few students with Air Ventures, I began working with Maritime Sales and Leasing, Inc on a regular basis.

David also had an awesome C310 where he and I did some Recurrent Training and some Cross-Country flying.

I later met the other Owner, John Bone who after a time decided to bring me on full time as a Pilot and Selling Aircraft.

As time went on, I made a lot of trips for them all over the Southeast and into the Caribbean with their aircraft.

Well, as Corporate jobs go, the owner decided to sell the C 421 and get on the list to purchase a brand new out of the factory CE 510 Citation Mustang.

I eventually sold the 421 to a company located in Alberta, Canada!

They didn't have a qualified Pilot at the time and as part of the deal, asked if we could deliver the aircraft. The owner agreed.

Of Course! Next sentence, John, "Tony, you think you can get the 421 to Alberta Canada?"

"Sure can John." Must have been a 'Can Do Spirit' talking as I knew that would be quite a trek.

MILK RIVER, ALBERTA, CANADA -

Now that's a jog for just about any aircraft from Newnan, Georgia however that turned out to be one of the most memorable flights ever.

I had a great 'Co-Pilot', my Wife, Judy, who had spent about two years in the right seat of our King Air, flown with me in all types of weather and into interesting destinations all over the West. Lately with the C 421, she'd flown with me on several occasions including flights into Florida, the Caribbean, and into the Appalachian Mountains.

I asked and she agreed to accompany me on this long and challenging Trek!

We methodically weighed and carefully loaded the extra tires, logbooks and everything we could find that went with the aircraft which left us a little room for our coolers, bags, etc.

Our route due to various weather systems was to Green River, Missouri, then Rapid City, South Dakota and from there to our final U.S. Stop, Great Falls Montana.

Yes, I applied just about everything I'd learned in the past about mountain flying into that trip.

We overnighted in Great Falls and had some delay for weather. We'd dodged a Cold Front passing overnight and were somewhat concerned about making it to our destination the next day.

The next morning, after our due diligence with Canadian Customs, worked out our flight plan and departed.

The weather front had just blown through that part of the country and weather reporting was sparse. It was extremely cold.

The first part of our flight we were on top of broken clouds but occasionally had good views of the countryside.

However, about half way to our destination, we encountered higher buildups with lenticular type clouds. Didn't expect this phenomenon at a mid-altitude.

Then working between the apparent mountain wave clouds, on top of one layer and below another, our flight became somewhat surreal visually.

Later Judy said she was praying all the way through that. I was just working my way through the mess.

We only picked up light rime ice. Turbulence wasn't too bad. Expected a lot worse.

Eventually we had better skies and could take in a little more scenery. However, I knew my 30-degree wind correction was there for a reason.

Finally called and spoke with ATF (Aerodrome Traffic Frequency - Unicom) at the small field. "We're clear down here however, snow on the runway and winds are terrible. Looks like about 40 across the runway."

OK... Short Field (2,900 Feet) – a little Snow on the runway – Winds Howling across the runway ... OK Looks like a dip into the old 'Alaska Experience Bucket' along with the Colorado Experience Bucket (Elevation – 3,500 Feet.)

Using the technique for radical crosswinds, not in the books... 'Utilize Trim. For instance, a left Crosswind (which it was) – Trim in a little left Aileron and a little right rudder to take some of the pressure off the controls.

As we turned final, we could see about 10 folks scurry outside the hanger watching. An Audience! Huddled just around the corner from the 45 knot winds with higher gusts. Now Blowing dust and rocks across the runway!

Wasn't sure what the betting was like. Whether we would make it or not.

Focused, I carefully touched on one wheel, held it straight and settled onto the runway. An amazingly perfect crosswind landing! No Brag. Just Fact. Had to brake quickly and held all the taxi crosswind techniques.

I managed to taxi over in front of the hangar somewhat out of the wind where the Customs Officer, dressed for the extreme cold, quickly came toward the aircraft. I opened the door and stepped back to let him pass forward to a seat, then closed the door hurriedly. He appreciated getting in out of the cold.

He was amazed I'd managed to land the aircraft in those conditions.

After a few questions and completing his checklist, he shook my hand, "Welcome to Canada!"

As Customs departed, one of the line guys stuck his head in and asked if we would taxi the aircraft down to another hangar so they could back the aircraft straight in.

I agreed, as it seemed their towing tug would not start due to the cold.

We started and taxied back out onto the runway – in the winds – then over to their other hangar, pulled around and stopped.

Shortly the big door opened and a smaller golf cart type tow eased us into the hangar. They closed the door, then we got out of the aircraft.

All the folks were very friendly and after a quick post flight, we pulled our bags and gear.

We were treated to coffee and donuts in their lounge while their maintenance department surveyed the logs and completed their inspection.

Shortly, we were getting into a waiting Suburban with the new owner and a friend and 5 hours later, arrived back in Great Falls, Montana.

Sure, hated to see the aircraft go. Certainly had enjoyed flying the 421. Quite an aircraft.

Cessna 421's are beautifully designed aircraft.

From there we took a rental car down to Salt Lake City, then Delta back home.

~

It would be some time before his new Mustang would be ready, however, it wasn't long before John and Dave put me together with another Part 135 Operator where shortly I found myself once again at FSI for Citation I and II which falls under the CE 550 Type Rating.

For those that do not know, CE 550 Type includes several other Cessna Jets including the Citation S-II, CE-500, CE -550, Citation Bravo, Citation V, CE-560 and possibly others. It doesn't include the Single Pilot Rating which is Optional. The CE-550 Type Rating is great one to have for moving up.

After another 135 Check Ride I was once again flying Jet Charters.

What a great aircraft to fly! Had a really great First Officer, Chris Pape, previously a Submarine Captain! Quite an interesting Cockpit I would say along with somewhat of a Paradigm Shift for Chris I'm sure. We had some great flights together and met and worked with many great folks.

NEXT AIRCRAFT – CITATION MUSTANG

About a year down the road, Maritime purchased the beautiful brand new out of the Factory Citation Mustang!

Of course, Flight Safety – Again. Not sure how many times I was there during my Career but a bunch.

It was a tough course to get through with all new state of the art Systems. (The aircraft was so new, there was somewhat of a struggle with their Instructors. Some were learning the aircraft at the same time we were.)

142

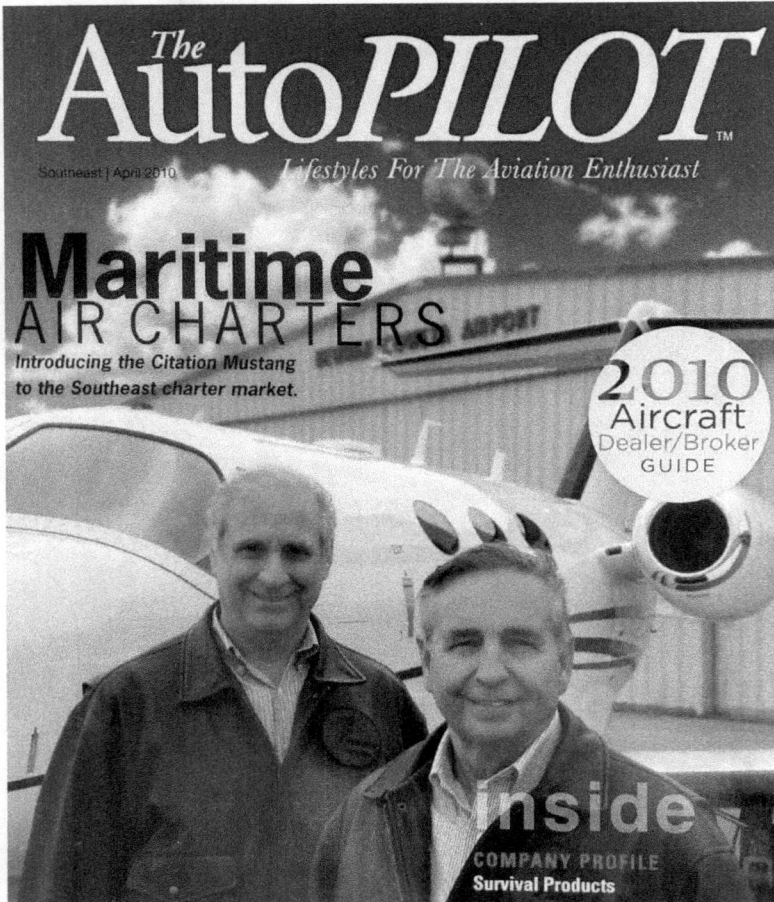

Raymond Foster on my right was a great Co-Captain with tons of experience in Aviation, including Scheduled Airline, 135 Charter, Flight Instruction and Naval Operations with 22 Carrier Landings!

I was certainly glad to have him aboard!

This turned out to be a great aircraft to fly and extremely comfortable traveling for pilots and Passengers.

Eventually, we stood it up on a Part 135 and flew the aircraft all over the U.S.

We had some awesome Passengers aboard!

Back to flying Flight Levels and IFR all the time.

Actually, it was a great feeling being back up where living was a lot easier. Except for Takeoff and Landings, we were simply managing the G-1000 and Auto-Pilot most of the time.

I really enjoyed the company of some great Co-Captains and Co-Pilots. Also, met and enjoyed some great times with several Celebrities.

We had wonderful times on occasion meeting Families of our Clients and were sometimes invited into their homes or offered free rooms at their condos.

Along the way I had many Single Pilot Operations and on occasion into some High-Density Airports. That flying of course is a little more intense. (Eventually I was qualified as a Citation Mustang Instructor.)

No Bravado here, just proud to be flying this Beautiful Machine!

I found for Single Pilot Operations in any aircraft, plan, plan, plan. However gets more important in King Airs and other Turbo Props but especially in Jets!

Things happen fast.

Have everything including possible alternates lined out before getting into the aircraft and everything you might need within hands reach once in the cockpit.

That includes expected approaches and alternates loaded into the 'Box' so to speak.

Our Mustang had the G1000 System with Synthetic Vision which was pretty darn nice Avionics. That could be a pretty easy jump for those that have been trained with the system even if in a Cessna 172!

Considering Synthetic Vision - I was on a really tight approach in moderate rain and relieved to get on the ground, then surprised by one of the customers, "Captain, that was a really nice flight. I was little concerned that we might not get in, then I could see the runway on your screen all the way down and figured we were ok." That happened several times.

Of course, you cannot use Synthetic Vision for your navigation, but it is helpful. We had good success through many rough weather flights. The aircraft handled icing conditions very well.

About the only downside of the aircraft was on arrivals at high density airports, especially with weather and with multiple, simultaneous approaches, etc.

ATC tended to keep us out of their normal Airline flow which was fine with us, however when very busy they can forget to hand you off.

That happened on at least two occasions, one at LaGuardia and once over Washington, D.C.

However, we were into Miami and others several times and we had no problems.

The other item was that the auto pilot had somewhat of a lag problem if approaching at speed, especially with a challenging angle. However, on a good note, the aircraft was very maneuverable... If you could read what was coming.

ATC at one of the heavily congested airports, asked on an ILS approach if I could maintain 200 KTs until intercept. I accepted although it would take a fairly steep turn. The trick I'd learned was to go to Heading Bug and Intercept the Localizer, stabilize then back to Nav. Otherwise, the autopilot was unable to capture and hold without overshoot. At a normal approach speed and angle NAV generally worked fine.

All in all, this was one of the aircraft I loved to fly.

In a way, I felt to be at the top of my game flying Single Pilot Jet and mixing it up with the best of the best.

~

After spending a couple of years in the Mustang with some great and memorable flights, John was Retiring and decided to sell all aircraft in the company's inventory.

Hey, it's a part of the general picture of Corporate and Part 135. Happens all the time.

I hated to see the Mustang go of course, along with some great Co-Pilots and Captains.

(Speaking of Copilots, I've been one of course and took on the role with a responsibility for Passenger Comforts and any other duties requested by the Captain along with pre-flight and in-flight duties of course.

Many times, you may be flying Co-Captain and switching outgoing legs and return legs with each taking on other tasks.

That system seems better than switching every other leg just for smoothness of operations.

Through the years you will establish friendships with some really great and interesting guys, (or ladies). Can't help but get to know someone when you have a lot of flying experiences along the way and eat a lot of meals together. You may develop a lifetime friendship with some. However, in Aviation it can be a little difficult to keep track of those Dynamic Souls - Aviators!)

John, Ray and I as Co-Captains had some awesome flights together during our time there.

I will always be grateful to Captain John Bone, the owner, and Maritime Air Charters for giving me the opportunity to work with them and to fly this magnificent Jet. It was the last Jet I flew during my 135 Career.

After selling the Mustang, I was offered to stay on and help sell the rest of the aircraft inventory. We together sold several, cleared everything and eventually the office was closed. Of course, everyone eventually moved on.

Working with Maritime was certainly one of the Highlights of my long career!

Next up –Back to Part 91 – Corporate

BARON!

One of our awesome Charter Customers happened to call me for a trip to New York whereas I hated to tell him we no longer had the Citation to fly.

He was bummed and so was I of course. He had been a great customer.

'Point' - Always treat your customers well. Treat them as your best friend. Go out of your way to always be ready in advance, ready to 'turn your prop' or 'light the fire'. Through the years, I've been hired by three of my Customers!

He owned a Cessna 182 and would like for me to get him current. I agreed and we had several flights to Florida and other destinations.

After a time, he found a BeechCraft Baron for sale and asked me to check it out. I did and then completed a pre-buy inspection at least to the point of legal and safe to fly to maintenance.

Once into Maintenance, an Annual was completed and it was soon ready for flight.

This Baron was one of my favorite aircraft to fly. Quiet, Plenty of power and comfortable for the passengers.

The aircraft really stood out on the ramp with the new paint and interior.

We had many enjoyable flights all over the U.S. including his New York Destinations, a little longer flight but without any problems.

SOME GENERAL NOTES ABOUT FLYING THIS AIRCRAFT...

Engine out's – not a problem. As with most Beechcraft the Aircraft is very well made, very strong on one engine and very stable.

However, an astute Pilot who has performed maneuvers in this aircraft, especially stall recovery knows that when full flaps are applied the aircraft, upon stall recovery will tend to pitch up. And, if not corrected can go to an extreme nose high situation. And, if in a go-around situation may pitch straight up and stall. Low to the ground of course is fatal.

We had just such a scenario at the LaGrange, GA airport a few years back.

With a Flight Instructor and his Student up front and a well-known Doctor in the back.

'Possibly' they were on the wrong frequency for the airport landing on the long runway.

Post-crash, the Glider Tow Pilot said he had announced a launch from the intersecting runway. (Final approach segments cannot be seen from either runway.)

It appears the Baron Pilot / Instructor saw the low flying Tow Plane at the last second, went to full throttle, went almost straight up, stalled and crashed on the runway.

If you get a chance to fly this great aircraft might practice stalls and go arounds. You'll quickly realize it takes a lot of yoke pressure to bring the nose down. Just be ready.

~

Well, a few years down the road and after some awesome times together, the owner's Company experienced some severe financial setbacks. That's Big Business sometimes...

Well, I ended up helping him sell both aircraft, then helped out in his multiple businesses for a while.

Once things were again stable, he had no interest in purchasing another aircraft.

So, once again, moving on.

BACK TO 135!

I once again, walked in and spoke directly with the President of a Company right back where I was an Instructor and had my original Flying Club... Falcon Field in Peachtree City!

It seems his Chief Pilot was retiring and asked if I would consider coming aboard in that regard.

I would, and soon completed my required training program and took my FAA Check Ride in their Cessna 421C.

The C 421C Model is an awesome aircraft to fly and very comfortable for passengers.

Once on line, had some great flights in that aircraft however, a few months along the way we ended up with some moderately severe maintenance problems.

The worst was a cracked internally heated windshield. Now that's a very spendy item, well north of $25,000 Dollars.

Maintenance found a short and burn in the internal wiring which possibly started the crack that expanded over time.

The aircraft would be down for weeks if not months.

Next was their King Air 90B which I'd been training in for my next Aircraft since their remaining King Air Pilot was moving on with another company.

Following some protracted maintenance issues, my King Air 90 FAA Check Ride date was set.

I was surprised when two FAA Examiners appeared and set up in our Conference room.

Uncomfortable of course, however, passed their extensive oral.

Then out to the aircraft with the Examiners began my Preflight Check.

Their questions were extensive which was not really a problem.

Taxiing out now I was quite relieved to be at this point. With thousands of King Air hours, I felt ready for anything.

However, on takeoff roll at about 80 Knots, Red Lights and loud Horn! Of course, I aborted. Perfectly. Nose wheel on centerline.

As I was slowing to a stop The Examiner behind me said "Very Nice Abort!"

Took the next turnoff and as we cleared the runway and stopped, the horn quit as well as the Warning Lights.

I began checking for possible problems and as I couldn't find anything, I asked the Examiner in the right seat., "Did you do something?

"I touched nothing!" he exclaimed.

Obviously, Back to Maintenance! 'Discontinuance' of course.

It turned out to be a faulty stall warning system problem.

As things turned out, that particular problem took about three weeks to correct. (Getting parts for these older B90 aircraft can be a problem.)

Following that repair and back on line, another major problem occurred. As I was flight testing the aircraft prior to continuing my Check Ride! - Auto Pilot Failure, This time a much more Severe and Costly problem.

This one turned out to require heavy maintenance, not just autopilot but Servos in the wing kind of replacements. Now set back at least another two months!

For the small company, that was a devastating blow.

Although the Owner worked hard and really tried to make it all work out financially, just couldn't happen. He was a great guy and I hated to see all the aircraft eventually sold and the company closed.

I really enjoyed flying with the other Pilots, working with our excellent Maintenance Department and had made a lot of Friends.

Right after that situation, the Pandemic Struck the U.S.

~

With the demise of that company, and as Flight Training slowly recovered, I once again began working in Aircraft Sales and Instructing and am still continuing that endeavor as of this writing.

By this time, we had sold our beautiful Lake front Home in LaGrange and purchased another closer to work with some decent equity gains. Time to retire? Maybe.

(However, some Insurance Companies these days seem to be controlling the state of one's capability to fly at a certain age across the board regardless of your Class 1 or 2 Medical, Experience, Record or Flying Capabilities).

Might want to keep that in mind and build in some decent Retirement Funds when you get near there. At least have a good Savings Account and Investments to get by the bumps and grinds of Part 135 as well as Corporate. Absolutely great jobs but as you can see following my tumultuous career, Financial Security may possibly be tenuous at times.

Do I have Millions in the Bank... Not quite, However,

I feel my greatest Success at this point lies well within my Adventure Packed Journey.

The Memorable Experiences, the Wonderful Fellowship of those who Shared my Journey, and just Moving About in the Freedom of Flight for over 50 years pretty much says it all.

CHAPTER 9

SOME FAVORITE AIRCRAFT TO FLY

Here I thought I'd throw in <u>some</u> of my own observations as a Pilot in regard to various Aircraft Designs and Companies.

I spent a lot of time in the Cessna 400 Series which could probably explain why I enjoy them so much. When you know pretty much all aspects of an aircraft very well perhaps is a good reason to like it.

BEGINNING WITH CESSNA ...

One thing I've always appreciated about Cessna Aircraft is their follow through on locations of everything from the instrument panel, side panels, power quadrants, etc.

Following the flow patterns from all the Cessnas I'd flown, it was an easy transition into the Conquest II Just a few more 'Clocks'. Then into the Citation II still not a lot of changes.

A few different instruments however practically all the Controlling Features and Flow Patterns still work!

CE 510 Citation Mustang

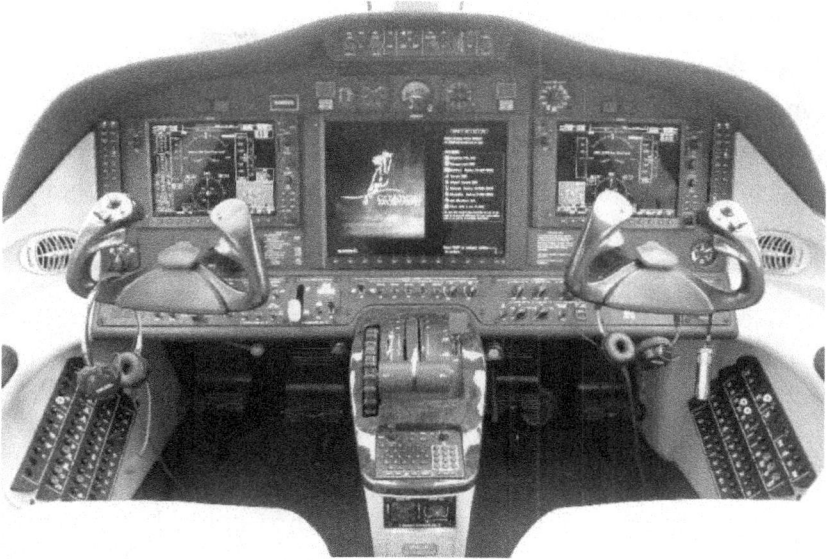

Similar but much larger TV Screens and less 'Clocks'

For Screen Size Perspective

Just kidding around about the clocks of course. What great Aircraft to fly!

Cessna 441 Conquest II – This is a 'Pilot's' plane. In other words, a real performer. Unlike the King Air PT 6 engines, they're not air driven. They have direct Axial drive with some Jet Thrust out the back. Power up... You're gone. No Spool up time required.

We sure liked the long range (2000 NM) and the 300 Knot Cruise at FL350. Actually, more like 280 Kts. for long range cruise economy.

We could make it from Anchorage to Seattle faster than our Citation due to their needed fuel stop.

Cessna 421 'Golden Eagle' – With the Geared Engines one has to utilize caution and slowly accelerate or decelerate. We never had a problem on any of our 421's but there have been some maintenance horror stories about.

Concerning Ice capabilities, I've had moderate to heavy icing in the 421B and 421C models and both have generally performed well.

However, for departures you have to use extra caution in extreme cold temperatures.

Example...Palwaukee, Illinois, Chicago Executive Airport, conditions were moderate snow with 10 below zero on the ground. After an Oil Congeal incident in Alaska, I was alert to watch oil temperatures and engine temps.

On our climb out, I shortly observed oil temp rising a little above and oil pressure a little lower than normal on my #1 engine. I alerted my Copilot that we may be returning for a landing and continued to watch any trends closely.

However, checking ambient temperatures ahead it seemed we would be in warmer conditions within a few minutes. All Instruments stayed within limitations. Luckily, we soon were in sunshine with the ambient air temperature rising. Shortly both engines were normal and we continued on to Atlanta.

Of course, descending utilize drag when you can to keep some power on the engines so as not to rapidly cool them down.

Cessna 402 - For any given aircraft, you have to realize its limitations.

In Alaska, our Cessna 402's were Specially Modified and Certified 'Known Ice'. However one really has to watch your ice buildups and simply know you're on your way down with a severe buildup. On one occasion I had unbelievable 'Antlers' building from the wingtips. I was 5 miles in trail of another Cessna 402 who'd just cleared the ridge adjacent to the Portage Glacier in Alaska and was cleared for the ILS in Valdez.

We were talking on our company frequency when he mentioned still getting some buffeting at 120 knots. My response, "Wayne, get the nose down to 140 knots." A minute later, "OK smooth now!"

Guess what, I descended at 140 knots as well with no problems.

It was amazing but both aircraft lost all ice and was dry when we landed at Valdez. It was 50 degrees on the surface!

One of the keys to handling the Cessna Twins is to keep your speed up.

They handle engine outs nicely if you keep your speed! If you don't, it can really bite you. Had the experience of one spool down on me at 50 feet, seconds after rotation from a short runway. Took some doing but managed to keep it out of the bushes for about 3 miles, then very slowly gained a little speed and eased it up enough to complete a very shallow turn back to the airport.

Brought one from the Alaska 'outback' with a very rough engine. Continually wanted to quit. However, when checking magnetos found it ran much smoother on the left magneto. So flew it about 100 Miles on one Magneto with almost normal performance. Made it just fine.

Cessna 310 – Not much to say here except watch your turns after landing. Some have made hard turns on rollout with terrible results. Easy to collapse that long Landing Gear in the turn. Best to stop completely then bring up a little power on the outside engine to turn off.

It's really a shame that Cessna is no longer building light twins. They're all aging aircraft and you might want to investigate maintenance records carefully.

PIPER TWINS

If you're just at the point for Multi-Engine Training today probably swing toward a Seminole (still in production). Or possibly an older Seneca will feel right for you. I've instructed in both and with good results.

The Apache is a great little twin for instruction, however they're much older aircraft, really look carefully at their maintenance history.

(It's <u>Not a good Plan</u> to train in any very old, poorly maintained aircraft just because it's cheaper.)

BEECHCRAFT TWINS

Leased back a Duchess for a couple of years. Never had any problems with training.

Barons are great aircraft but a little fast for general Multi-Instruction. However, sure enjoy flying them!

CESSNA SINGLES

All good flying aircraft. Best Stick and Rudder instruction aircraft.

Only lost one engine completely. Maintenance generally reported they were an easier aircraft to work with.

(Cessna 152 – Dead stick to an old dirt strip a few miles from Anchorage.)

One of the items I appreciated in Cessna's over some of the others is the two doors. There's more comfort of course getting in and out.

Also, one might consider it as a safety issue in deplaning in case of fire or following an emergency landing.

In both Piper and Cessna I suppose it's a good idea to keep them closed and secure for an off airport landing simply for structural integrity. However, might consider cracking a door so as not to get trapped in the aircraft. (Your Leatherman Tool or Heavy Duty similar device should be on your Belt for those type emergencies.) Some say to have a small hammer along as well.

One of course has to adjust your procedures and techniques with every aircraft.

I can say the Cessna 182 as well as the C 206 are two of the best work horses around.

PIPER SINGLES

Great Aircraft to fly. With tons of time in pretty much all models, I rarely had a maintenance problem. Air Conditioning was at times very helpful of course.

BEECHCRAFT SINGLES - QUIETEST OF ALL. GOOD SOLID
AIRCRAFT.

In Closing, One answer to our shortage of Future American
Pilots could be that at least one of the big American owned
Aircraft Companies come up with a program such as existed
in the 1980's and 1990's.

For instance, Beechcraft's Club Pro Program was oriented
to Sales of course, but dovetailed in with local Beech Aero
Clubs and Flight Schools. Cessna is the closest to have
accomplished something similar but there's still more work
to be done.

Although it's more profitable for corporations these days
to produce Turbine and Jet Aircraft, and continue to ignore
the Flight Training situation, perhaps someone in
management should consider what it's doing to the integrity
and strength of Aviation in America.

BeechCraft, Cessna or Piper, Salt of the earth in American
Aviation, Please step up to the Plate and provide us with
another Club Program and at least one or two 'Competitive'
Training Aircraft.

As a pilot, you might consider whatever you fly, drive or
use daily. See who owns the company you're supporting.

Diamond Aircraft are not American made by the way.

I've got about 250+ hours in Diamonds, ok to fly but can be
a little uncomfortable in Summers around here. You would
think in today's world someone would come up with a light
weight Air Conditioning unit for all our Training Aircraft!

Just a note, about all the Turbo-Prop and Turbo-Jet time
I've had along the way. They're very Quiet, Comfortable, and
Dependable. Never had an engine problem... The End.

CHAPTER 10

GOLDEN RULES – HIGH OR LOW COUNTRY

These TEN GOLDEN RULES apply to any of Your Flying!
One of these rules may simply save your life someday.

GOLDEN RULE 1

REMEMBER - OXYGEN! (NOT THE O2 KIND.)
Just as the briefing goes on the airlines – Place the mask on yourself, breathe normally, and then help others! If you go under you can't help anyone.

A Captain's Decision – 'Living' Decisions

On occasion you may have to wake up with a remorseful thought for a while concerning decisions made especially when working as a Medevac Pilot. Yes, you may wake up somewhat remorseful, but Y<u>ou Wake Up</u>. The ones you saved also wake up!

There are no remorseful thoughts about any other actions taken as a Charter or Commuter Pilot in situations where you have to downsize your load, block a passenger from boarding, miss a pickup due to weather, etc. "Sorry, we can't pick you up today but possibly tomorrow afternoon if the weather cooperates." etc.

Be aware however, there may be a circumstance where you have to make a life-or-death decision concerning others.

Oxygen!   *Stay alive to save others.*

GOLDEN RULE 2

DECISION MAKING RULE
Resist external pressures

OK You're a million miles from nowhere. You as Pilot in Command are the Captain of your Ship! You make the Decisions.

In that process forget Passenger, Company, Boss, Financial, Client or Get-Home Pressures. None of these should weigh in to your decision to go or not go, to land or not land, to fuel or not take on fuel.

None of those factors will keep you alive. However, any one of those factors can sure be the end of you and your passengers.

Seems like a no brainer, however possibly hundreds of aircraft have gone down due to a Pilot succumbing to one or two of these pressures.

You may disappoint people with your decisions, cause them to change plans, frustrate them to no end. "Gonna' miss my connecting flight!"

Sometimes making the right decision can cost you a good client or possibly your job. There's other clients and other jobs.

"What do you mean we can't take three of our coolers?" "Look there's plenty of room for them."

"I spent a lot of money on this fishing trip." On and on…

Another comment, "We flew out of here OK last year!"

Beware – it's usually one ignorant loud voice that's trying to lead everyone else into Heaven's gate a little early.

Pilots have acquiesced and attempted such ridiculous feats based on a loud customer claiming they had done it before. Take my advice, don't die today trying to please your clients!.

As professional Pilots we're trained to make our decisions based on operational factors such as weather, equipment, Pilot readiness and our experience level and to operate within legal parameters.

Your decisions in all Operations have to be based on those same Operational, Legal, and Personal Limitations!

Evaluating Risk Factors is a key part of flying anytime.

If, after discussing the aspects your passengers are still not satisfied with the plan, they don't have to go along with it! Go home, or remain where they are. They can wait another day or find another company.

MISSION PRESSURE

Early on, you want to have set your own limitations about weather, departure, enroute and destinations.

The variables are things to scrutinize, measure, double check, etc.

Your aircraft numbers are solid. Don't stretch over into the gray side.

One thing to really watch for in flying Scheduled or On-Demand Charter is to realize you're under Mission Pressure quite often.

Of course, consider all the items courteously and understand that these things can add up.

Don't let your customer(s), or your employer press you into something you're not comfortable about!

Through the years I've encountered all types of pressure from aircraft loads to 'Gotta' get there by 11, to what do you mean Bob can't go with us? Or Sorry sir, you'll have to leave your cooler of Salmon.

On a call out one night, after reviewing the weather at the airport, I decided not to go.

My employer was highly agitated over my decision as these were very important people and they needed to get down to the valley tonight!

Night – Low ceiling – Snowing - Icing Forecast – Surrounded by mountains –

The owner arrived and in a grumbling tone said weather's fine! Guess I'm going to have to get another Pilot, Blah, Blah, Blah.

Well, sure enough he boarded our people, and taxied out into the night.

I of course was quite concerned.

I hung around for a while thinking about where I was going next to look for work.

Shortly after their departure I stepped out of the office onto the ramp and heard an aircraft engine turning up some incredible RPMs.

I thought there would be a loud explosion in short order but lo and behold things quieted down and suddenly there was a landing light on final.

They landed, taxied in, shutdown, doors opened and passengers bailed out, grabbed their briefcases, and headed toward their cars.

Not much was said as I assisted in parking and tying down the aircraft. Then in a grumbling tone, "Dam Ice!"

I seemed to still have my job.

Don't bend your 'Limitations' or your aircraft 'Numbers' for Customers or Company!

GOLDEN RULE 3

ALWAYS LEAVE YOURSELF AN 'OUT'

This is a basic rule and generally speaks for itself.

All instructors should be identifying for their students the 'Outs' available to meet every possible abnormal or emergency operation during their early days of training.

For instance, on climb out from your airport, what would you do if you lose an engine – Fly straight ahead and land in the trees? Or turn left 20 degrees and land in the spacious field?

I usually took a little longer in soloing my students just to ensure for the pattern regime they knew how to handle every emergency and knew every possible out available to them.

In that regard, I observed a U-Tube video the other day with a very confident and seemingly knowledgeable instructor demonstrating to his new student what to listen for right after takeoff? He lifted the nose until he got a solid stall warning horn... On Takeoff! At about 200 feet. I guess he missed the Wind Shear Chapter as well as never dreamed he could have an engine barf right at that moment. There's a reason for the 1500 Foot rule folks and that is to Leave Yourself an 'Out'. You cannot use the altitude above you when falling.

They survived thus the video. However, the next step in the chain is that the student with his new license shows this to his girlfriend or three buddies on a humid day with thunderstorms in the vicinity - a setup for disaster.

Leaving yourself an out may simply be height above Terra Firma when performing maneuvers. An inadvertent stall spin low to the ground can ruin a good day of flying.

Also, always respect your IFR minimums. They're there for a reason.

However, in Alaska especially, I realize there are a lot of one-way airports whereas you're landing against a mountainside etc. That possibly is the only exception once you're committed.

Having been into and out of some of the most dramatic one-way airstrips in Alaska I learned to make a sound plan for escape at different distances. Once you're down below your escape routes and committed, you're only out may be to focus on your approach and landing and especially focus on your airspeed to control your landing distance.

Analyze Take off & Landing Wind Direction carefully.

GOLDEN RULE 4

PLAN AHEAD FOR DIFFERENT SCENARIOS

Fly like a Professional even if you have no plans to do so.

Don't be surprised when something goes wrong. Plan for those scenarios and be quite surprised when everything goes as planned.

As mentioned earlier consider the winds aloft above and below your planned altitude especially in mountainous terrain. Consider them in relation to what you would do with an engine out or other emergency situation or having to climb to get over icing in unexpected cloud tops.

So, you're only flying at 5,000 feet and nowhere near the peaks of the mountains off to the east and not really concerned about the winds at 10,000 and 12,000.

Well... If the peaks are parallel to your course of flight and perpendicular to the wind direction at those peaks you could encounter some severe rotor clouds, mountain waves and other forms of clear air turbulence.

One of the hardest jolts I've gotten into was flying a Seneca from Anchorage to Palmer, Alaska on a nice clear day. Winds at the surface were light. I was fairly new to the area, winds aloft for 3 and 6 thousand were forecast 15 knots and out of the Northeast.

As I flew approximately past Birchwood, I encountered gut wrenching up and down drafts, hit my head and promptly dropped my seat and tightened my belt. The next jolt cracked one of the rear windows. Flying attitude and a low power setting I eventually got clear.

Know your aircraft's power settings for level, climb, and descent scenarios. You may not be able to depend on your airspeed indicator or other static instruments in this situation.

The turbulence I encountered was from high wind turbulence spilling off the Chugach Mountain range, a phenomenon I later learned was fairly common in the Anchorage area.

Think 'What ifs' such as flying home multi-engine with an engine caged. Terrain is 10,000 along the route. Look at altitudes required, possible landing strips and weather along your planned route. What's the temperature at your planned altitude and weather possibilities such as Ice?

Alright, it's minus 25 at 12,000 feet. Heater failure? Can you and your passengers make it should that happen? Got any survival gear such as blankets aboard.

Just Think... What ifs?

GOLDEN RULE 5

FOLLOW COMMON AND SPECIFIC RULES AND PROCEDURES ALWAYS

Many airports are non-controlled. Use caution, be vigilant, communicate, and utilize proper entry and departure procedures even if you think you're the only aircraft in the area.

In that regard, <u>never taxi into position and hold at a non-controlled airport</u>. Sitting with your back to the final approach corridor waiting for an aircraft to clear or to complete a takeoff run is <u>not a good practice</u>. Sure, you observed no one on final just before you pulled out. However, what about the hard to see Cessna 310 approaching on a straight in Final? What if he had lost radios or switched to the wrong frequency when handed off by approach. What if the fellow downwind abeam had an engine failure and did not see you as he was watching the aircraft on takeoff roll, then in a panic state forgot to announce his intention to land – while you're sitting there blind to the final approach corridor.

That's especially true at Runways acceptable for Jet Traffic which are faster and typically tracking the localizer on a straight in approach even in VFR Conditions.

I almost experienced a fist fight in a terminal after a Falcon Captain had to twice go around due to two Diamond aircraft pulling out in front of his approach! At least there was only screaming and yelling involved. (That's costly to Jets!)

Stay on the Defensive at all times.

photo courtesy VansAirForce.net

The Classic High Wing Low Wing Incursion on Approach

Also, at non-controlled airports, be ready for another Pilot to make an illegal and unthinkable move and enter your flight path on takeoff or landing. I had such an experience and near miss with a brightly colored 'no-rad' bi-wing sport plane.

Although announcing my positions for landing in the left traffic pattern, on very short final the aircraft pulled onto the runway right in front of me. I was in a Cessna 402B at approach speed with gear and full flaps.

I powered up and moved to the right at low level, announced my 'go around' and began cleaning up my aircraft while keeping the aircraft in sight. Suddenly, the aircraft went to a right oblique climbing turn right in front of my windshield!

I had no choice but to dive toward the runway in a hard-left turn passing underneath the aircraft!

He passed above me, seemingly oblivious that I was even there!

GOLDEN RULE 6

UP HIGH, LEARN TO READ THE STORMS and TOPS OF BUILDUPS IN YOUR PATH

'Cumulonimbus Mammatus Insipidus'
Learned that one from Meteorology Class

Just kidding about this one. Tops were reported by a military aircraft above 100,000! My right Nacelle is at the bottom of picture. We're at FL 250 Conquest II. Mt. Spur Volcanic Eruption,-Alaska of course.

Best go well around if you can. Tops were +/- 100 miles across. Rocks were falling from the sky!

This view as we're deviating with ATC which we can generally do. Read those tops. If the top of the storm is Fuzzy you can probably penetrate easily with a light bumpy ride. If the top is really sharp, smooth against a blue sky, it's building with strong vertical drafts. Best to avoid that one

DOWN LOW   SIMPLY DO NOT SCUD RUN AS A NORMAL PRACTICE

It will eventually get you.

One of my best Students amazingly committed to his Private, Commercial, and Multi-Engine Training was a 709 Ride Candidate who under Part 135 landed his perfectly good Cessna 207 with six aboard, yes in the flat tundra. It seems that the FAA frowns upon such doings.

He explained to me he'd been between the villages many times at that altitude feeling his way back and forth.

However, this one time... perhaps it was indeed colder than most days whereas his aircraft's <u>actual altitude</u> was lower than indicated.

Regardless, he was totally surprised when he contacted Terra Firma. White out, Gray out, Flat Light - it doesn't matter. Scud running as a normal practice is not a good plan.

The case is that some weather phenomenon has a way of bending light rays and obscuring or disguising familiar terrain features.

One of our 402's came back from a mail run with limbs from a treetop stuck in the wheel wells. That Pilot survived his scud running incident, learned his lesson and vowed to never try it again.

It's not just us GA Pilots that sometimes are guilty. A Mark Air Boeing 737 on a deadhead leg, landed 2 miles short of the destination runway after getting a 'lowest descent vector' in a nearby valley, then attempted to scud run to the airport.

At Prudhoe Bay, a Military C130 landed on the downwind leg in a 'flat light' incident.

All these incidents were in familiar territory along a repeated route.

Scud Run Roulette is Not a good plan for a <u>long Flight Career</u> or for a long life for that matter.

Continuously monitor your altitude requirements!

GOLDEN RULE 7

RESOURCE MANAGEMENT

Use all information and resources available to you.

You always want to talk to other Pilots who may have experience in your planned destination area.

Cross Check Instruments.

If flying a two-Pilot crew, remember there's no place for exaggerated Egos in the cockpit.

Plan to take a Crew Resource Management Class which also includes Single Pilot Resource management.

Single Pilot Resource Management may include help from a passenger or passengers.

Here's such an incident...

Alaskan Nights are very dark so always be prepared for a Power Failure.

This incident occurred on takeoff on a very dark and dreary night with 1,000 overcast and about 2 miles visibility.

I'd just gotten into the air when just prior to 'Gear Up' a loud 'Pop', everything went dark. No panel lights and all instruments were dark. No gear lights, no cabin lights.

I had my hand on the gear switch but caught myself before cycling and left the gear in place.

I pulled the flashlight (always within reach at night) to see my instruments and began a right turn back around to the airport. All that is somewhat of a challenge to say the least. Luckily, I had a female passenger in the right seat who offered and courageously assisted me by holding the flashlight on the instruments.

It was dark, very dark. She also helped me run through the emergency checklists as I had my hands full of airplane. Nothing worked. I primarily focused on simply flying the aircraft and maintaining contact with the runway.

I flew a standard pattern keeping the runway lights in sight and looked to the tower for landing clearance. On the downwind I looked and observed no other aircraft on final. I continued around on a modified base leg. Now the runway was fully illuminated and yes indeed, a bright Green Light was now emitting from the tower. I suspected they saw my lights disappear on takeoff. With this steady handed passenger's assistance, we were almost home. I think her name was Julie.

We were not out of the woods yet with no landing lights, no electrical instruments and especially no gear lights. I luckily hadn't cycled the gear after takeoff so I reasoned they were still down and locked. However, still a little disconcerting.

I planned to be as smooth as possible and be prepared for the worst.

Squeaking the Mains on - Normal touchdown, now the nose wheel, yes.... Normal.

Flashing Green was now coming from the tower and I taxied to the gate.

GOLDEN RULE 8

FLY – NAVIGATE – COMMUNICATE

This is your order of Priorities. You've heard that time and time again. Keep these in order and you'll have a much better chance of surviving in this business.

FLY!   AIRSPEED, AIRSPEED, AIRSPEED!!!

For instance, one of my questions about crashes where Pilots die usually with someone else aboard is "Why were they talking to ATC instead of getting themselves out of the situation".

A horrid example is that of a Pilot and his wife aboard a Cherokee Six on fire at 2,000 feet and calling for help on the radio. They eventually crashed – Two Fatals.

<u>PUT THE AIRCRAFT ON THE GROUND NOW!</u> From that altitude that can happen in less than 20 seconds!

Dive in a slip, fly any altitude, any configuration, any airspeed <u>required to Position Yourself on Short - Short Final</u> with full drag configuration if possible. Get to proper landing speed even if it's a crash landing. Get clear of the aircraft. Deal with the rest later.

Always Fly First. Maintain control of your aircraft.

I've always taught 'Crash Management' Techniques. I know of one of my past students that survived along with his three passengers when his engine quit right after takeoff. Suddenly quiet at about 400 feet. With no fields ahead, he made a slight turn and put it between the two largest trees and let the aircraft take the brunt of the Energy. They all walked away.

Another note, always make sure you're at the slowest ground speed at contact with Terra-Firma! In general, Stay aware of the current wind direction and of course land into the wind. A downwind touchdown energy of impact increases three-fold!

ATC communications are excellent 99.9 % of the time where things are handled well and safely.

However, knowing exactly where you are at all times should become a natural trait.

Trust controllers to a point, a point where you feel things might not be as they should. Remember it's ok to question an assigned runway, altitude or vector or any instruction if you feel there's a problem or better option.

'Flying off their assigned screen on a busy day' can cause such a problem. I've been on a vector more than once and with no heading changes from ATC saw (VFR conditions) or in IMC Conditions knew I was being vectored into high terrain. On one particular day in California in an IFR on top condition, I continued on an assigned vector, arrived and called in close to the mountain side just to make a point. Of course, a 'pause', then a quick turn by ATC. They do get busy so know where you are at all times. Be aware of improper clearances, vectors or early descent altitudes! All have happened along the way.

Know where you are at all times. Legal may not equate to safe.

"If a Pilot makes a critical mistake, the Pilot dies. If the Controller makes a critical mistake, the Pilot dies."

Know where you are at All Times!

Also Remember, they cannot help you with an onboard fire or damaged aircraft. <u>Take care of it yourself.</u> Get the aircraft on the ground or on the surface of the water!

Just keep that in mind. Only you are responsible for you.

GOLDEN RULE 9

BE PREPARED TO SURVIVE ON YOUR OWN.

If you're in mountainous or sparsely populated areas, departing for a destination outside of the immediate area of any of the cities, be ready to survive. A Human 'Bean' is quite low on the natural food chain.

This means having a means to last several days with no outside help. Planes have a way of disappearing.

On <u>every</u> flight carry with you at least some basic items to help you last a few days.

Dress appropriately or have available clothing, boots, gloves and waterproof gear.

If you're simply up and down flight instructing it's wise to keep a few items in your flight bag as well. In the wilderness, it's a good idea to carry a mosquito net as there are some areas where the mosquitos and black flies will literally eat you alive.

Another is a couple of large heavy duty rolled up Black Trash Bags for protection from sudden inclement weather or slogging through snow or mud or simply for additional survival gear, etc.. I simply rolled up 3 and stuck them in my pilot bag. (Weighs nothing) Carry with them 5 Bungies. You can simply use two small ones for your feet and legs by wrapping around your ankle area and a little longer one around your leg above the knee and hooked to your longest bungie around your waste or belt. If it's rocky or slippery use caution of course. For upper body simply cut a space for your head at the bottom of the bag and arm holes at your shoulder height. May look dumb but you'll be dry and warm!

This simple tactic for survival will help preserve body heat and keep you dry. Hypothermia is not a joke!

Have along some type of safe fire starter. How about a small bag or two of Fritos – excellent fuel to establish a good camp fire. Just strike a match to a pile and experiment yourself. Don't use them all at once as about 10 chips will burn for 5 minutes. You can eat the other 45. Not bad to get a few carbos and a little grease in you. They take up very little space and <u>weigh nothing</u>.

On flights into remote areas or in any mountainous country I recommend complying with the areas published survival gear requirement and carrying a good survival Weapon.

GOLDEN RULE 10

ALWAYS BE <u>WHERE YOU ARE</u>.

HAVE PRESCENCE OF MIND DURING YOUR PILOT DUTIES.

Pilots need to have a solid presence of mind on all phases of flight especially during critical regimes of flight. However,

For instance – While hurriedly moving automatically through your preflight, someone watching asks you a question. Best to stop what you're doing, answer the question, and then resume your preflight focus. Talking and moving through your preflight may leave a section blank in your memory or possibly cause you to forget something.

"Did I replace the oil cap securely? Did I actually check it?"

Ever have that gnawing feeling? If so, best to get out the ladder and check it again.

Did I ensure the nose baggage door was locked? Better check it.

Rushing along can also cause you to skip a checklist item and may very well begin an accident chain. Especially have presence of mind in subfreezing temperatures of your aircraft's condition or configuration of critical items like your Flap and Fuel Selector settings for takeoffs and landings.

The next item tends to fall somewhere between distractions and common sense. That is when a Businessman, Doctor or other Professional has the finances to afford a nice high-performance aircraft for his travels. I've flown with and trained several.

When they check in with some aircraft salesmen whose theory is, "You might as well buy and train in the aircraft you want to be traveling in." and they follow their lead, they start out with a Handicap. I think that many accidents involving those folks are caused by gaps in training and lack of stick and rudder skills and experience as an airman in general.

I say to those buying an aircraft for personal travel, get some training in various related aircraft to the one you intend to purchase. Work your way through for instance several Cessna Singles and Twins before you climb into a Cessna Conquest II or Citation Mustang!

Also, after you've completed training for your aircraft, if you haven't already, attain some additional training through other courses such as Mountain Flying or Aerobatic training.

Another very important additional safety precaution for the new aircraft owner is to have an Instructor or safety Pilot with high time in the right seat especially in marginal weather or into unfamiliar airports or terrain.

Another Phenomenon I discovered flying right seat as an Instructor or Safety Pilot with professionals, whether businessmen, political types, contractors or doctors is that they can 'Leave' the cockpit mentally. I've found that for instance a businessman is speaking at a meeting shortly after arrival or is a contractor submitting a bid by noon, etc., that many times 20 - 30 minutes out from landing they can leave the cockpit mentally and if alone could end up a statistic.

It's not just those folks who can leave the cockpit a little early. Pilots including professionals can be out there as well.

Always 'Be Where You Are!

Here's another item to consider that can lead us any of us into oblivion.

How about the devices we carry today?

Don't let your 'devices' interrupt your process during any phase of flight.

Just because the general public is 'dumbing and numbing' due to all their devices doesn't mean we as Pilots have to succumb to it.

Be careful folks. Don't be 'dumbed down' by these devices to the point of not knowing where you are when your screen goes blank and to the point of losing common sense.

Be Where You Are. Be With Who You Are With.

Yes, utilize the latest technologies but attempt to balance it against the world outside of that realm. Do not become so addicted that you cannot function otherwise and miss out on the reality of your situation.

'ALWAYS BE <u>WHERE YOU ARE</u>.'

It's very important especially when Piloting an aircraft! Don't get locked into any device and forget to look outside. **Fly your aircraft. Be Vigilant.**

SOME PRACTICAL ONE LINERS AND NOTES TO LIVE BY

1. <u>GREEN LIGHT FOR LANDING</u>

We all are taught Gas, Undercarriage, Mixtures, Props

Well, Add one more verbal call on Short Final.

"GREEN LIGHT FOR LANDING"

Just a glance is all it takes, You'll <u>never</u> have an accidental Gear up Landing if you add that to your Verbals!

2. **<u>Maintain Airspeed</u>** even if you're flying a BRICK! That stall warning means lower the nose! Adjust you're A.O.A right before touchdown land or water.

3. **<u>Always be correcting</u>**. You're in a Fluid Environment with continual change. Small, early change pressures are required for the smoothest flight.

4. **<u>Always keep your mind on your task of flying</u>**, not a business meeting, not a dinner engagement, not a ball game.

5. **<u>Fly, Navigate Communicate</u>**! So many still have this wrong. Don't be stressing over the radio when you need to get on the ground safely.

6. **Always leave yourself an 'out'** – Your 'out' should be planned well before beginning your takeoff or landing or traveling enroute especially for night flight over mountainous terrain.

7. **Don't run out of Fuel!** Always have a good reserve. (Mentioned because it's still goes on.) Don't trust whoever you delegated to fuel, a Lineman, First Officer or someone else. Learned that lesson early on. When overfueled, underfueled, or wrongly fueled. The Wrong fuel didn't happen to me but on occasion Jet A has been applied to Cessna 421s, etc. In other words, if you're Pilot in Command, Observe all your Fuelings.

8. **Weight and Balance** - Always, Always <u>Ensure personally</u> you're within. Don't guess or totally trust a Lineman or Maintenance. It's awfully embarrassing to Crash Land right after rotation! I was aware of two incidents both loaded too heavily with Aft C.G. Both crashed on runway. Guess who's responsible in the FAA's eyes. P.I.C. of course.

9. **Below DH or MDA – Don't Press It.** The rules are out there for a reason. One of the worst – Get Home 'Itis' happens often. Many times it's just a Flight Crew heading home after a drop-off. Happened right here at our local airport. Both good pilots that went below MDA searching for the runway, landed a King Air 200 in trees a mile from the runway. Fatal.

10. **Have your Emergency Memory Procedures down pat.** I also recommend be able to do everything with your eyes closed, be able to find those Emergency

Items, O2 masks and know how to select 100% Oxygen, gear and flap selectors, include Critical Circuit Breakers (I use a feel and count across and down system). Just takes some practice of course. Be able to utilize all flight controls and in short be able to control your aircraft. With personal experience of an explosive decompression, I try to push this type of training. Mine was at 25,000 feet. Dust and Fog was incredible. Could not see or hear my Co-Pilot! Went through the whole Emergency Descent procedure and was headed down in seconds. It was + / - 3 minutes before the cockpit and cabin air began to clear.

11.**Night Flying** – Put those phones away. A flash from a phone camera can cause blindness! There's been fatal accidents in that regard.

Question for my Students...You're Night Flying, clear night, you've got some lights in your windshield not moving, a Red and Green with no Landing light. It's not moving. A Green light is on the right side, a Red light is on the left. Still not moving. (Of course, teach to change something quickly by slightly turning and move those lights to another place on your windshield or if closer put the lights in your side window. Maintain control of the situation and don't lose sight of the other aircraft.

Question – (Green light is on the right side, a Red light is on the left) Is the aircraft coming toward you or going away from you? Again, most Blog answers on the Internet are incorrect. Most say 'Going Away' obviously. Wrong. It's coming toward you. Why you ask... Well the Wingtip Nav Lights are generally Shielded from the back!

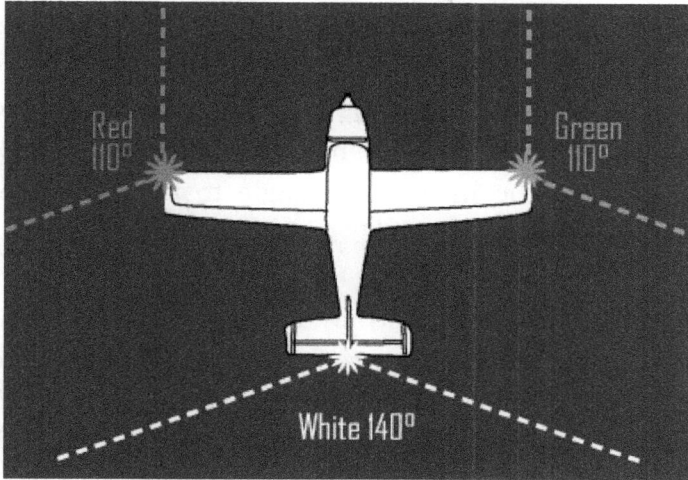

Very rare of course, but sometimes a pilot or even a maintenance person may unintentionally put the lens back on the wrong wings. Personal experience again. I followed one such aircraft to the airport and approached the Pilot on the ramp. We both checked and he was totally surprised, "Holy Cow! I changed those yesterday! Put the lens on the wrong wings!" (Regretfully there's a lot of fellows posting Incorrect Aviation 'knowledge' on U Tube, etc. talking about when the aircraft is going away from you, you see red on your left and green on your right when you should see a white tail light, beacon or strobes only.

12.**IFR To Minimums** – On an ILS or any approach when Approaching Minimums take note of your wind correction angle. Adjust your view for the Runway accordingly. The tendency is to look straight out the windshield. Crabbing right look slightly left, Crabbing left, look slightly right. On one instance as we were nearing ILS minimums, my Co-pilot was straining for the runway and could not see it. We were in moderate rain and also in heavy wind gusts, however the airport was reporting 500 and 1 1/2 miles visibility. I glanced up, nothing, then back <u>at my wind correction angle</u> and realized to look far to the right, there it was in my right-side window! in plain sight! I continued the heavy crab angle to a normal landing position.

13.**<u>Hand Prop</u>** – Regretfully there are still accidents in this regard. We taught it religiously in Alaska. However, not many have received practical training these days. Always have a qualified person at the controls if you perform it or teach it. The largest aircraft I've started this way was a Cherokee Six. It was a task for sure but necessary at the time. Of course a trusted Pilot was at the controls.

14. **Watch your passengers carefully**. We had a recent Fatal where a Passenger walked into an operating prop. That's <u>totally uncalled for</u>. The pilot left the engine running to deplane his two passengers??? <u>Never do that</u>! Always shut down before deplaning. Or if shut down is totally not possible (dead battery in Alaska at 55 below zero), have a second pilot, get out and control the passengers safely away from the aircraft. Also, Really watch and control Children to ensure they do not run under a wing or around the aircraft regardless if engines are running or not running. If a high energy child runs into an exhaust or pitot tube your whole day could be ruined, leave a mark on them and your reputation.

CHAPTER 11

SEE SOME COUNTRY

One of the things I've often been asked is where all have you flown. So, thought I'd summarize by listing the destination airports straight out of my Logbook. Took some time of course.

DESTINATIONS, ARRIVALS AND DEPARTURES

OF

Tony Boyd Priest, ATP – CFI-II, MEI, as Pilot in Command
Verified through Log Book Entries
(Additional takeoffs and landings at the same Airports, Alaskan Beaches, Lakes, Rivers, Gravel Bars, Roads, and Unimproved Strips are not listed.)

1.	KPOC	Brackett Field, Pomona, CA
2.	KEMT	El Monte Apt., El Monte, CA
3.	KCNO	Chino Apt., Chino, CA
4.	KFUL	Fullerton Muni Apt., Fullerton, CA
5.	KVNY	Nan Nuys Apt., Nan Nuys, CA
6.	KBNG	Banning Muni Apt., Banning, CA
7.	KBFL	Meadows Field, Bakersfield, CA
8.	KCCB	Cable Apt., Upland, CA
9.	KCRQ	McLellan-Palomar Apt., Carlsbad, CA
10.	KAVX	Catalina Apt., Avalon, CA
11.	KRIR	Flabob Apt., Riverside/Rubidoux, CA
12.	KSNA	John Wayne Apt., Santa Ana, CA
13.	KBFL	Meadows Field, Bakersfield, CA
14.	L05	Kern Valley Apt., Kernville, CA
15.	KLAS	Las Vegas McCarran, Las Vegas, NV

16. KHMT   Hemet-Ryan Apt., Hemet, CA

17. KL38   San Juan Capistrano, CA (Closed)

18. KRAL   Riverside Muni Apt., Riverside, CA
19. KSBA   Santa Barbara Muni Apt., Santa Barbara, CA
20. KNTD   Ventura County Apt., Point Mugu, CA
21. KSZP   Santa Paula Apt., Santa Paula, CA
22. KWJF   General Wm J Fox Airfield, Lancaster, CA
23. KSAN   San Diego Int. Apt., San Diego, CA
24. KHII   Lake Havasu City Apt., Lake Havasu City, AZ
25. ZZYX   ZZYZX - Soda Springs Apt. CA. (Closed)
26. KEED   Needles Apt., Needles, CA
27. KWHP   Whiteman Apt., Los Angeles, CA
28. KMYV   Yuba County Apt., Marysville, CA
29. KTVL   Lake Tahoe Apt., South Lake Tahoe, CA
30. KNOW   Port Angeles CGAS, Port Angeles, WA
31. KLGB   Daugherty Field, Long Beach, CA
32. KNOT   Ontario Int. Apt., Ontario, CA
33. KOAK   Metropolitan Oakland Int. Apt., Oakland, CA
34. KAPV   Apple Valley Apt., Apple Valley, CA
35. L26   Hesperia Apt., Hesperia, CA
36. KSAN   San Diego Int. Apt., San Diego, CA
37. KREI   Redlands Muni Apt., Redlands, CA
38. L22   Yucca Valley Apt., Yucca Valley, CA
39. KSMO   Santa Monica Apt., Santa Monica CA
40. KPSP   Palm Springs Int. Apt., Palm Springs, CA

41. KFFC   Falcon Field, Peachtree City, GA
42. 7A5   Roanoke Muni Apt., Roanoke, AL
43. KCCO   Coweta County Apt., Newnan, GA
44. KCTJ   Carrollton Apt., Carrollton, GA
45. KLGC   Lagrange Apt., Lagrange, GA
46. 6A2   Griffin-Spalding Apt., Griffin, GA
47. KFTY   Brown Field, Fulton County Apt., Atlanta, GA
48. KAUO   Auburn-Opelika Apt., Auburn, AL
49. KCSG   Columbus Apt., Columbus, GA
50. KUOS   Franklin County Apt., Sewanee, TN
51. KAGS   Augusta Apt., Augusta, GA
52. KABY   Albany Apt., Albany, GA
53. KMLJ   Baldwin County Apt., Milledgeville, GA
54. KFRP   St Lucie County Int. Apt., Ft Pierce FL
55. KMCN   Middle Georgia Regional Apt., Macon, GA
56. KHXD   Hilton Head Apt., Hilton Head Island, SC
57. KICT   Wichita Apt., Wichita, KS
58. KATL   Hartsfield Jackson, Atlanta, GA
59. KPDK   DeKalb- Peachtree Apt., Atlanta, GA
60. 32GA   Sebastian Cove Apt., Eatonton, GA
61. KEUF   Weedon Field Apt., Eufaula, AL
62. KMOB   Mobile Regional Apt.., Mobile AL
63. 91GA   Flying Frog Field Apt., Moreland, GA
64. KTLH   Tallahassee Regional Apt., Tallahassee, FL
65. KPBF   Grider Field, Pine Bluff, AR
66. KAXS   Altus Muni Apt., Altus, OK
67. KAMA   Amarillo Int. Apt., Amarillo, TX
68. KABQ   Albuquerque Int. Apt., Albuquerque, NM
69. KWWR   West Woodward Apt., Woodward, OK
70. KPHX   Phoenix Sky Harbor Int. Apt., Phoenix, AZ
71. KSKX   Taos Regional Apt., Taos, NM
72. KMLC   McAlester Regional Apt., McAlester, OK
73. KHOT   Memorial Field Apt., Hot Springs, AR
74. KASN   Talladega Muni Apt., Talladega, AL
75. KPIM   Pine Mountain Apt., Pine Mountain, GA
76. KBHM   Birmingham Apt., Birmingham, AL

77. KAYS   Waycross-Ware County Apt., Waycross, GA

78. KAVL   Ashville Regional Apt., Ashville, NC

79. KRMG   Richard B Russell Apt., Rome, GA

80. KDHN   Dothan Regional Apt., Dothan, AL

81. KOPN   Thomaston-Upson County Apt., Thomaston, GA

82. KCHA   Lovell Field Apt., Chattanooga TN

83. KACJ   Souther Field Apt., Regional Apt., Americus, GA

84. 6A1   Butler Muni Apt., Butler, GA

85. KHKY   Hickory Reg. Apt., Hickory/Beech Mtn. NC

86. KTOC   Letourneau Field Apt., Toccoa, GA

87. RGNT   Grants-Milan Muni Apt., Grants, NM

88. KCVC   Covington Muni Apt., Covington, GA

89. KCLT   Charlotte/Douglas Int. Apt., Charlotte, NC

90. 4A4   Cornelius Moore Field, Cedartown, GA

91. KRYY   Cobb County Apt., Marietta, GA

92. KPYP   Centre-Piedmont CO. Regional Apt., Centre, AL

93. D73   Monroe-Walton County Apt., Monroe, GA

94. KGLH   Greenville Mid Delta Apt., Greenville, MS

95. KMKJ   Mountain Empire Apt., Marion, VA

96. KRBD   Dallas Exe. Apt./Red Bird Field, Dallas, TX

97. KCH   Charleston AFB/Int. Apt., Charleston, SC

98. 4A7   Atlanta South Regional Apt., Hampton, GA

99. KLZU   Gwinnett County Apt., Lawrenceville, GA

100.3J7   Green County Reg. Apt., Greensboro, GA

101.KSCD   Merkel Field, Sylacauga Muni, Sylacauga, AL

102.KSSI   Malcolm McKinney Apt., Brunswick, GA

103.F47   St. George Apt., St George Island, FL

104.KAAF   Apalachicola Regional Apt., Apalachicola FL

105.FA43   Dog Island Apt., Carrabelle FL

106.KNEW   Lake Front Apt., New Orleans LA

107.KFRP   St Lucie County Int. Apt., Ft Pierce FL

108.MYGF   Grand Bahamas Int. Freeport, Grand Bahamas

109.KRIC   Capital Regional Apt., Richmond VA

110.KEWR   Newark Liberty Int. Apt., Newark NJ

111.KTUL   Tulsa Int. Apt., Tulsa OK

112.KPXE   Perry-Houston Apt., Perry, GA

113.KTRI   Tri-Cities Regional Tn/VA Apt., Bristol, TN
114.KBKL   Raleigh County Memorial Apt., Beckley, WV
115.KOWB   Owensboro-Daviess Co. Apt., Owensboro, KY
116.KSGF   Springfield Apt., Springfield, MO
117.KMKC   Wheeler Downtown Apt., Kansas City, MO
118.KCKB   North-Central West VA. Apt., Clarksburg, WV
119.KCLE   Cleveland-Hopkins Int. Apt., Cleveland, OH
120.KMEM   Memphis Int. Apt., Memphis, TN
121.KBKW   Raleigh County memorial Apt., Bleckley, WV
122.KBLF   Mercer County Apt., Bluefield, WV
123.K18A   Franklin County Apt., Canon, GA
124.KPFN   Panama City, Florida
125.KAGC   Allegheny County Apt., Pittsburg, PA
126.KGRI   Central Nebraska Rgnl. Apt. Grand Island, NE
127.KMGR   Montgomery Regional Apt. Montgomery, AL
128.KJAX   Jacksonville Apt., Jacksonville, FL
129.KMIA   Miami Int. Apt. Miami, FL
130.L35   Big Bear Apt., Big Bear Lake, CA
131.KBUR   Bob Hope Apt., Burbank, CA.
132.KTOA   Zaperini Field, Torrance, CA
133.KRAL   Riverside Muni. Apt., Riverside, CA
134.KCSB   Cambridge Muni. Apt., Cambridge, NE
135.KAPA   Centennial Apt., Denver, CO
136.KSJC   Norman Y Mineta, San Jose Int., San Jose, CA
137.KLBG   Daugherty Field Apt., Long Beach, CA
138.KLAX   Los Angeles Intl. Las Angeles, CA
139.KSBO   Emanuel County Apt. Swainsboro, GA
140.KSTK   Sterling Muni Apt. Sterling, CO
141.KAJO   Corona Muni, Corona, CA
142.KOXR   Oxnard Airport, Oxnard, CA
143.KMRY   Monterey Peninsula, Monterey, CA
144.KTNP   Twenty-Nine Palms, 29 Palms, CA
145.KHHR   Jack North Rod Field, Hawthorn, CA
146.KTLR   Mefford Field, Tulare, CA
147.KRAL   Riverside Muni, Riverside, CA
148.KBAK   Columbus Muni, Columbus, IN

149. KCOM — Coleman Muni, Coleman, TX
150. KRED — Red Lodge Apt., Red Lodge, MT
151. KTSP — Tehachapi Municipal Apt., Tehachapi, CA
152. KSPA — Downtown Memorial, Spartanburg, SC
153. KHHR — Jack Northrop Field, Hawthorne, CA
154. KHMT — Hemet-Ryan Apt., Hemet, CA
155. KBVU — Boulder City Muni, Boulder City, NV
156. KOKB — Ocean Side Municipal, Ocean Side, CA
157. KMYF — Montgomery Field, San Diego, CA
158. KNYL — Yuma M.C. Air Sta./Yuma Int., Yuma, AZ
159. KCRQ — McClellan-Palomar, Carlsbad, CA
160. KCCB — Cable Apt., Upland, CA
161. KO54 — Lonnie Pool Field, Weaverville, CA
162. KRBL — Red Bluff Muni, Red Bluff, CA
163. KCPM — Compton Woodley Apt., Compton, CA
164. KSFO — San Francisco Intl, San Francisco, CA
165. KWJF — General W Fox Airfield, Lancaster, CA
166. KBHC — Baxley Muni, Baxley, GA

167. L16 Meadow Lark Apt., Huntington Beach, CA (Closed)

168. KHII — Lake Havasu City Muni., Lake Havasu, AZ
169. KVGT — North Las Vegas Apt., Las Vegas, NV
170. KRNO — Reno/Tahoe Intl, Reno, NV
171. KELY — Ely Apt./Yelland Field, Ely, NV
172. KSGU — St. George Apt., St. George, UT
173. KGUP — Gallup Muni. Apt., Gallup, NM
174. KTVL — Lake Tahoe Airport, South Lake Tahoe, CA
175. KTPH — Tonopah Apt., Tonopah, NV

176. PANC   Anchorage Int., Anchorage, AK
177. KGAL   Edward G Pitka Sr Airport, Galena, AK
178. PAMR   Merrill Field, Anchorage, AK
179. PENA   Kenai Muni, Kenai, AK
180. PTKA   Talkeetna Apt., Talkeetna, AK
181. PABV   Birchwood Apt., Birchwood, AK
182. PAKN   King Salmon Apt., King Salmon, AK
183. PTYE   Tyonek Apt., Tyonek, AK
184. PAKY   Karluk Apt., Karluk, AK
185. PADQ   Kodiak Apt., Kodiak, AK
186. PAWS   Wasilla Apt., Wasilla, AK
187. PCDV   Merle Smith Apt., Cordova, AK
188. PAFS   Nikolai Apt., Nikolai, AK
189. PANI   Aniak Apt.., Aniak AK
190. PVDZ   Valdez Pioneer Field, Valdez, AK
191. PEDF   Elmendorf Air Force Basse, Anchorage, AK
192. PMCG   McGrath Airport, McGrath, AK
193. PCKD   Crooked Creek Apt., Crooked Creek, AK
194. KRDV   Red Devil Apt., Red Devil, AK
195. PSLQ   Sleepmute Apt., Sleepmute Village, AK
196. PHCR   Holy Cross Apt., Holy Cross, AK
197. PANV   Anvik Apt., Anvik Village, AK
198. PKGX   Grayling Village Apt., Grayling, AK
199. PSHX   Shageluk Village Apt., Shageluk, AK
200. PBET   Bethel Apt., Bethel, AK
201. PKLG   Kalskag Village Apt., Kalskag, AK
202. Z40   Goose Bay Apt., Goose Bay, AK
203. PRSH   Russian Mission Apt., Russian Mission, AK
204. PDUT   Dutch Harbor Apt., Dutch Harbor, AK
205. PACD   Cold Bay, AK
206. PAKA   Tatitlek, AK
207. Z55   Lake Louise, AK
208. PASV   Sparrevohn LRRS, AK
209. 2AK   Lime Village, AK
210. PATL   Tatalina LRRS, Takotna, AK
211. PARY   Ruby Apt., Ruby, AK

212.PAAQ   Palmer Municipal Airport, Palmer, AK
213.D.O.T. Farewell Apt., Farewell, AK
214.4AK6   Wolf Lake Apt., Palmer, AK
215.PAFS   Nikolai Apt., Nikolai, AK
216.PANU   Nulato Apt., Nulato, AK
217.PABT   Bettles Apt., Bettles, AK
218.ORT   Northway Apt., Northway, AK
219.PATE   Teller Apt., Teller, AK
220.3AK5   Drift River Apt., Drift River, AK
221.PASC   Prudhoe Bay Deadhorse Apt., Deadhorse, AK
222.PADL   Dillingham Apt., Dillingham, AK
223.PANO   Nondalton Apt., Nondalton, AK
224.AK04   Pedro Bay Apt., Pedro Bay, AK
225.KNK   Kokhanok APT., Kokhanok, AK
226.PAPH   Port Heiden Apt., Port Heiden, AK
227.PAGS   Gustavus Apt., Gustavus, AK
228.PAPE   Perryville Apt., Perryville, AK
229.PAKK   Akhiok APT., Akhiok, AK
230.PACH   Chuathbaluk Apt., Chuathbaluk, AK
231.PAEM   Emmonak Apt., Emmonak, AK
232.PAFA   Fairbanks Intl. Apt, Fairbanks, AK
233.PAGA   Edward Pitka Sr. Apt., Galena, AK
234.PAHO   Homer Apt., Homer, AK
235.PALH   Lake Hood Airport, Anchorage, AK
236.PBGQ   Big Lake Apt., Big Lake, AK
237.PSWD   Seward Apt., Seward, AK
238.PAGK   Gulkana Apt., Gulkana, AK
239.KCSR   Campbell Airstrip, Anchorage, AK
240.6AK5   Fire Island Apt. Anchorage, AK
241.Point   McKenzie Apt., AK (Closed)
242.PAGQ   Big Lake Apt., Big Lake, AK
243.PAQY   Girdwood Apt., Girdwood, AK
244.5HO   Hope Apt., Hope, AK
245.PASO   Seldovia Apt., Seldovia, AK
246.PAMD   Middleton Island Apt., Middleton, AK
247.D.O.T. Johnston Point, Hinchinbrook Island, AK

248.PAYA   Yakutat Apt., Yakutat, AK
249.KPVU   Provo Municipal Apt, Provo, UT
250.PASW   Skwentna Apt., Skwentna, AK
251.PASA   Savoonga Apt., Savoonga, AK
252.PADK   Adak Apt., Adak Island, AK
253.PAIW   Wales Apt., Wales, AK
254.PAAK   Atka Apt., Atka, AK
255.PAOT   Ralph Wien Memorial Apt., Kotzebue, AK
256.PAPO   Point Hope Apt., Point Hope, AK
257.PASN   St. Paul, St. Paul Island, AK
258.PABE   Barter Island LRRS, Barter Island, AK
259.PAEI   Eielson AFB, Fairbanks, AK
260.ATU   Casco Cove C.G. Sta., Attu Island, AK
261.CYDA   Dawson City Apt., Dawson City, YT
262.CYXY   Erik Nielsen Int., White Horse, Yukon Territory
263.PABR   Wiley Post – Will Rogers Mem., Utqiagvik, AK
264.POME   Nome Apt., Nome, AK
265.PAM   Indian Mountain LRRS, Utopia Creek, AK
266.PASI   Sitka Rocky Gutierrez Apt., Sitka, AK
267.PAP   St. George Apt., St. George Island,
268.PALU   Cape Lisburne LRRS Apt., Cape Lisburne, AK
269.PAYA   Yakutat Apt., Yakutat, AK
270.PDLG   Dillingham Apt., Dillingham, AK
271.PAII   Egegik Apt., Egegik, AK
272.D.O.T.   Red Dog Mine, AK (Pvt.)
273.PA79   Chignik Lake Apt., Chignik, AK
274.6R7   Old Harbor Apt., Old Harbor, AK
275.PAKH   Akhiok Apt., Akhiok, AK
276.PAOU   Nelson Lagoon Apt., False Pass, AK
277.PALJ   Port Alsworth Apt., Port Alsworth, AK
278.PANO   Nondalton Apt., Nondalton, AK
279.PAWG   Wrangell Apt., Wrangell, AK
280.PASX   Soldotna Apt., Soldotna, AK
281.PADK   Adak Island Apt., Adak Island, AK
282.PAFA   Fairbanks Intl., Fairbanks, AK
283.PKTN   Ketchikan Apt., Ketchikan, AK

284.PAWD   Seward Apt., Seward, AK
285.PABG   Beluga Apt., Beluga, AK
286.PAKU   Ugnu-Kuparuk Apt., Kuparuk, AK
287.PAJN   Juneau Int., Juneau, AK
288.PCDB   Cold Bay Apt., Cold Bay, AK
289.PIGG   Igiugig Apt., Igiugig, AK
290.PSDP   Sand Point Apt., Sand Point, AK
291.PAIL   Iliamna Apt., Iliamna, AK
292.PBFI   Boeing Field/King County Int., Seattle WA
293.CYZF   Yellow Knife Airport, North West Territory, YK
294.KBJC   Jeffco Apt., Broomfield, CO
295.KAPA   Denver Centennial, Denver, CO
296.KOKC   Will Rogers World, Oklahoma City, OK
297.KSDL   Scottsdale Apt., Scottsdale, AZ
298.KFNL   Fort Collins-Loveland Muni., Loveland, CO
299.KSEA   Seattle Tacoma Int., Seattle WA
300.KRIL   Garfield County Rgnl, Rifle, CO
301.KPUB   Pueblo Memorial, Pueblo, CO
302.KRAP   Rapid City Rgnl, Rapid City, SD
303.KAJZ   Blake Field Airport, Delta, CO
304.KGJT   Grand Junction Rgnl, Grand Junction, CO
305.KLAA   Lamar Muni, Lamar, CO
306.K8V7   Springfield Muni, Springfield, CO
307.K2V5   Wray Muni, Wray, CO
308.KSYF   St. Francis, Cheyenne County Muni., KS
309.KPRB   Paso Robles Muni. Apt., Paso Robles, CA
310.KHEQ   Holyoke Apt., Holyoke, CO
311.KTQK   Scott City Muni, Scott City, KS
312.KALS   San Luis Valley Rgnl/Bergman, Alamosa, CO
313.KDEN   Denver Int., Denver, CO
314.KASE   Aspen-Pitkin Co/Sardy Field, Aspen, CO
315.SDO1   MJ Aviation Apt., Mitchell, SD
316.KOKS   Garden County Apt., Oshkosh, NE
317.KMWA   Veterans Apt. of Southern Illinois, Marion, IL
318.KOGA   Searle Field, Ogallala, NE
319.KCPR   Casper/Natrona Co. Int. Apt., Casper WY

320.KTEL	Perry County Muni, Tell City, IN
321.KLBB	Lubbock Preston Smith Intl. Lubbock, TX
322.KEGE	Eagle County Rgnl, Eagle, CO
323.KCBK	Shalz Field, Colby, KS
324.KMVI	Monte Vista Muni, Monte Vista, CO
325.KGGF	Grant Muni, Grant, NE
326.KOJC	Johnson County Executive, Olathe, KS
327.KOMA	Eppley Airfield, Omaha, NE
328.KFSD	Joe Foss Field, Sioux Falls, SD
329.KFAR	Hector Intl, Fargo, ND
330.KMSO	Missoula Intl, Missoula, MT
331.KPGA	Page Muni, Page, AZ
332.KBIL	Billings Logan Intl. Billings, MT
333.KBFF	Western Nebraska Rgnl/Heilig, Scotts Bluff, NE
334.KBFI	Boeing Field, Seattle, WA
335.KBOI	Boise Air Terminal, Boise, ID
336.KLNK	Lincoln Apt., Lincoln, NE
337.KHDN	Yampa Valley, Hayden CO
338.KDPA	DuPage Apt., Chicago, IL
339.KJAC	Jackson Hole Apt., Jackson, WY
340.KSBS	Bob Adams Apt., Steamboat Springs, CO
341.KDRO	Durango-La Plata County, Durango, CO
342.KLHX	La Junta Muni, La Junta, CO
343.KSNY	Sidney Munt/Lloyd Carr Field, Sidney, NE
344.KOWA	Owatonna Rgnl, Owatonna, MN
345.KQ39	Mineral County. Apt., Creede, CO
346.KBAK	Columbus Municipal Airport, Columbus, IN
347.KAIA	Alliance Muni, Alliance, NE
348.KGRR	Gerald R Ford Int. Apt., Grand Rapids, MI
349.WY11	A Bar A Ranch Apt., Encampment, WY
350.KMVL	Morrisville/Stowe State, Morrisville, VT
351.KTUS	Tucson Intl, Tucson, AZ
352.KGXY	Greeley/Weld County, Greeley, CO
353.KTAD	Perry Stokes Apt., Trinidad, CO
354.KDLN	Dillon Apt., Dillon, MT
355.3KY9	Miles Field Apt., Shelbyville, KY

356.KCAG   Craig/Moffat Apt., Craig, CO
357.KAVK   Alva Regional Apt., Alva, OK
358.K74V   Roosevelt Muni, Roosevelt, UT
359.KTEX   Telluride Rgnl, Telluride, CO
360.KCDS   Childress Muni. Apt., Childress, TX
361.KSAF   Santa Fe Muni, Santa Fe, NM
362.2VG2   Upperville Apt., Upperville, VA
363.KAUS   Austin/Bergstrom Intl, Austin, TX
364.KSLC   Salt Lake City Intl., Salt Lake City, UT
365.U07   Bullfrog Basin Apt., Glen Canyon Rec. Area, Utah
366.KBYG   Johnson County Apt., Buffalo, WY
367.U64   Monticello Apt., Monticello, UT
368.KGNB   Granby Grand County, Granby, CO
369.KLIT   Adams Field, Little Rock, AR
370.KIDP   Independence Muni., Independence, KS
371.KTWF   Joslin Field/Magic Valley Rgnl, Twin Falls, ID
372.KONL   O'Neill Muni. Apt., John L Baker Fld., O'Neill, NE
373.KMAF   Midland Int., Midland, TX
374.KGUC   Gunnison/Crested Butte Rgnl, Gunnison, CO
375.KASE   Aspen/Pitkin County/Sandy Field, Aspen, CO
376.KHOE   Homerville Apt., Homerville, GA
377.KTCC   Tucumcari Muni, Tucumcari, NM
378.KKNB   Kanab Muni, Kanab, UT
379.KBCE   Bryce Canyon Apt., Bryce Canyon, UT
380.KOLU   Columbus Muni, Columbus, NE
381.KSTL   Lambert-St Louis Intl, St. Louis, MO
382.KSHR   Sheridan County Apt., Sheridan, WY
383.KDGW   Converse County Apt., Douglas, WY
384.KTOR   Torrington Muni, Torrington, WY
385.K2V6   Yuma Muni, Yuma, CO
386.KDAY   James M Cox Dayton Intl, Dayton, OH
387.KMW   Veterans Apt. of So. Illinois, Marion, IL.
388.KCOS   Colorado Springs Muni, Colorado Springs, CO
389.KCGS   College Park Apt., College Park, MD
390.KPEQ   Pecos Muni, Pecos, TX
391.KASG   Springdale Muni, Springdale, AR

392.KAJZ   Blake Field Apt., Delta, CO
393.KUTA   Tunica Muni. Apt., Tunica, MS
394.KGLD   Goodland Field/Goodland Muni, Goodland, KS
395.KIWS   West Houston Apt., Houston, TX
396.KITR   Kit Carson County Apt., Burlington, CO
397.KRWL   Rawlins Muni/Harvey Field, Rawlins, WY
398.KBBW   Broken Bow Muni, Broken Bow, NE
399.KWRL   Worland Municipal, Worland, WY.
400.KTUP   Tupelo Regional, Tupelo, MS.
401.KMTJ   Montrose Regional, Montrose, CO
402.KISN   Sloulin Field Intl, Williston, ND
403.KMPE   Philadelphia Muni, Philadelphia, MS
404.KTYS   Mc Ghee Tyson Apt., Knoxville, TN.
405.KCSG   Columbus Metro, Columbus GA
406.KMEI   Key Field, Meridian, MS.
407.KJKA   Jack Edwards, Gulf Shores, AL.
408.KGVL   Lee Gilmer Memorial, Gainesville, GA.
409.KCLT   Charlotte/Douglas Apt., Charlotte, NC.
410.KDCU   Pryor Field, Decatur, AL.
411.KAGS   Augusta Regional at Bush Field, Augusta, GA.
412.KCRW   Yeager Apt., Charleston, WV.
413.KEWR   Newark Liberty Int., Newark NJ
414.KTVI   Thomasville Regional, Thomasville, GA
415.KLNA   Palm Beach County Park, West Palm Beach, FL.
416.KSAV   Savannah/Hilton Head Intl, Savannah, GA.
417.KBNA   Nashville Intl, Nashville, TN.
418.KCRG   Craig Muni, Jacksonville, FL.
419.KMKL   McKeller-Sipes Regional, Jackson, TN
420.KONX   Currituck Co. Regional., NC
421.MYAM   Marsh Harbor Apt. Bahamas
422.KGTF   Great Falls Regional, Great Falls, MT
423.KCGI   Cape Girardeau Rgnl. Apt., Cape Girardeau, MO
424.CEK6   Killam-Sedgewick Apt., Killam, Alberta, CA
425.KBHM   Birmingham-Shuttlesworth, Birmingham, AL
426.KOKV   Winchester Regional, Winchester, VA
427.KRIC   Richmond Intl, Richmond, VA

428.KPFN   Bay County Int., Panama City, FL
429.KDFW   Dallas/Fort Worth Intl, Dallas-Fort Worth, TX
430.KJZI   Charleston Executive, Charleston, SC
431.KEVV   Evansville Regional, Evansville, IN
432.KZZV   Zanesville Muni, Zanesville, OH
433.KBQK   Brunswick Golden Isles Apt., Brunswick, GA
434.KGPT   Gulfport-Biloxi Intl, Gulfport, MS
435.KDQH   Douglas Mini, Douglas, GA
436.KDNL   Daniel Field, Augusta, GA
437.KDHN   Dothan Regional, Dothan, AL
438.KVLD   Valdosta Regional, Valdosta, GA.
439.KCHS   Charleston AFB/Intl, Charleston, SC
440.KTMA   Henry Tift Myers Apt., Tifton, GA
441.KPAH   Barkley Regional, Paducah, KY
442.KIPJ   Lincolnton Lincoln Rgnl. Apt., Lincolnton, NC
443.KRST   Rochester Intl, Rochester, MN
444.KAPA   Centennial Apt.., Denver CO
445.KGTR   Golden Triangle Regional, Columbus, MS
446.K2J2   Liberty County Apt., Hinesville, GA.
447.KLOU   Bowman Field, Louisville, KY
448.KJVY   Clark Regional, Jeffersonville, IN
449.KSGT   Stuttgart Muni., Apt., Stuttgart, AR
450.KORL   Executive Apt., Orlando, FL
451.KVDI   Vidalia Regional, Vidalia, GA
452.KJAN   Jackson-Evers Intl, Jackson, MS
453.KOKZ   Kaolin Field, Sandersville, GA
454.KJQF   Concord Regional, Concord, NC
455.KDAB   Daytona Beach Int., Daytona Beach FL
456.KXFL   Flagler County Apt., Palm Coast, FL
457.KTPA   Tampa Intl, Tampa, FL
458.KROC   Greater Rochester Intl, Rochester, NY
459.KDCA   Ronald Reagan Washington Intl, D.C., VA
460.KABY   Southwest Georgia Regional, Albany, GA
461.KBWI   Baltimore/Washington Intl, Baltimore, MD
462.MS96   Barrett Field Apt., Philadelphia, MS
463.KCAE   Columbia Metropolitan Apt., Columbia, SC

464.KMDW   Chicago Midway Intl, Chicago, IL
465.KPXE   Perry-Houston Apt.., Perry GA
466.KLUK   Cincinnati Muni Apt. Lunken, Cincinnati, OH
467.KTBR   Statesboro-Bullock County, Statesboro, GA
468.KOM   Eppley Airfield, Omaha, NE
469.KCRE   Grand Strand Apt., North Myrtle Beach, SC
470.KMAC   Macon Downtown Apt., Macon, GA
471.KHUM   Houma-Terrebonne Apt., Houma, LA
472.KDCU   Pryor Field Regional, Decatur AL
473.KAVL   Ashville Regional, Ashville, NC
474.KTVI   Thomasville Regional, Thomasville, GA
475.KLOZ   London-Corbin Apt... Magee Field, London, KY
476.KLFT   Lafayette Regional, Lafayette, LA
477.KUNK   Unalakleet Apt., Unalakleet, AK
478.KVAY   South Jersey Regional, Mt. Holly, NJ
479.K15J   Cook County Apt., Adel, GA
480.KMCO   Orlando Int., Orlando, FL
481.KSEF   Sebring Regional Apt., Sebring, FL
482.KHSV   Huntsville Intl-Carl T Jones F, Huntsville, AL
483.KPIE   St Petersburg-Clearwater Intl, Clearwater, FL
484.KMMU   Morristown Muni. Apt., Morristown, NJ
485.KMVC   Monroe County Apt., Monroeville, AL
486.KBED   Laurence G Hanscom Field, Bedford, MA
487.KUOX   University-Oxford, Oxford, MS
488.KVDF   Tampa Executive, Tampa, FL
489.KDAL   Dallas Love Field, Dallas, TX
490.KUZA   York County/Bryant Field, Rock Hill SC
491.KRYV   Watertown Muni. Apt., Watertown WI
492.KINT   Smith Reynolds, Winston Salem, NC
493.KHQU   Thomson-McDuffie County, Thomson, GA
494.KLAL   Lakeland Linder Regional, Lakeland, FL
495.KX60   Williston Muni, Williston, FL
496.KALX   Thomas C Russell Field, Alexander City, AL
497.KGYH   Donaldson Center, Greenville, SC
498.KTEB   Teterboro Apt., Teterboro, NJ
499.KELP   El Paso Intl, El Paso, TX

500.KISM   Kissimmee Gateway, Orlando, FL
501.KPWK   Chicago Executive, Prospect Heights, IL
502.KSBM   Sheboygan County Memorial, Sheboygan, WI
503.KALB   Albany Int., Albany, NY
504.MWCR   Owen Roberts Int., Grand Cayman
505.KFLL   FT. Lauderdale Intl, Fort Lauderdale, FL
506.KBOW   Bartow Exe. Apt., Bartow, FL
507.KIXD   New Century Air center, Olathe, KS
508.35X   Triple Ace Field, Decatur, TX
509.MYNN   Lynden Pindling Int., Nassau, Bahamas
510.KGSO   Piedmont Triad Intl, Greensboro, NC
511.KMMU   Morristown Mini, Morristown, NJ
512.KIAD   Washington Dulles Int., Washington DC, VA
513.KGTR   Golden Triangle Rgnl, Columbus, MS
514.KSTC   St Cloud Regional, St Cloud, MS
515.KCPT   Cleburne, Regional Apt., Cleburne, TX
516.KMCI   Kansas City Int., Kansas, MO
517.KHOU   William P Hobby, Houston, TX
518.KLWB   Greenbrier Valley Apt., Lewisburg, WV
519.KAIK   Aiken Muni, Aiken, SC
520.KHEF   Manassas Regional/H.P. Davis, Manassas, VA
521.KDWH   David Wayne Hooks Memorial, Houston, TX
522.LRM   La Romana Apt., La Romana, Dominican Rep
523.KSOP   Moore CO. Apt., Pinehurst/Southern Pines, NC
524.KLHZ   Franklin County Apt., Louisburg, NC
525.KFMN   Four Corners Regional, Farmington, NM
526.KSIK   Sikeston Memorial Muni, Sikeston, MO
527.KLKR   Lancaster County-Mc Whirter, Lancaster, SC
528.KSWF   Stewart Int., Newburgh, NY
529.KCUB   Jim Hamilton L.B. Owens, Columbia, SC
530.KVVS   Joseph A Hardy Connellsville, Connellsville, PA
531.KIAH   George Bush Int., Houston, TX
532.KGTR   Golden Triangle Regional, Columbus, MS
533.KPIR   Pierre Regional, Pierre, SD
534.KBDL   Bradley Intl. Airport Bradley, CT
535.KPWK   Chicago Exe. (Palwaukee) Wheeling, IL

536.KMDW   Chicago Midway Int., Chicago IL
537.KSGJ   St. Augustine Apt., St. Augustine, FL
538.KCGI   Cape Girardeau Regional, Cape Girardeau, MO
539.KECG   Elizabeth City CG Regional, Elizabeth City, NC
540.KDFI   Defiance Memorial, Defiance, OH
541.KOPF   Opa-Locka Executive, Miami, FL
542.KMLB   Melbourne Int., Melbourne, FL
543.KVRB   Vero Beach Muni, Vero Beach, FL
544.KPBI   Palm Beach Int., West Palm Beach, FL
545.MYRP   New Port Nelson Apt., Port Nelson, Bahamas
546.MYNN   Lynden Pindling Int., Nassau Bahamas
547.MBPV   Providenciales Intl. Apt., Turks and Caicos Isl.
548.MDLR   La Romana Apt., Dominican Republic
549.TKPN   Nevis Island Apt., Newcastle, Nevis Island, DWI
550.TIST   Cyril E King Virgin Islands Apt., St Thomas, VI
551.SJU   Luis Munoz Marin Int. Apt. San Juan Puerto Rico
552.KHRL   Valley Int., Harlingen, TX
553.KCYS   Cheyenne Regional/Jerry Olson, Cheyenne, WY
554.KPGV   Pitt-Greenville Apt., Greenville, NC
555.TSIG   Isle Grande, San Juan Puerto Rico
556.KBOS   General Edward Lawrence Logan, Boston, MA
557.KAPF   Naples Muni, Naples, FL
558.KSAT   San Antonio Int., San Antonio, TX
559.KGKT   Gatlinburg-Pigeon Forge Apt., Sevierville, TN
560.KVDF   Tampa Executive Apt., Tampa, FL
561.KCLW   Clearwater Air Park, Clearwater, FL
562.KDTS   Destin-Fort Walton Beach Apt., Destin, FL
563.K51A   Hawkinsville-Pulaski CO. Apt., Hawkinsville, GA
564.KDNN   Dalton Muni, Dalton, GA
565.KFSM   Fort Smith Regional, Fort Smith, AR
566.CYBW   Calgary Springbank Apt., Calgary, Alberta, CA
567.CYQL   Lethbridge Apt., Lethbridge, Alberta CA
568.KRSW   Southwest Florida Int., Fort Myers, FL
569.KHDI   Hardwick Field, Cleveland, TN
570.KROA   Roanoke Regnl.Woodrum Field, Roanoke VA
571.KORH   Worchester Regional, Worcester, MA

572.KLEX   Blue Grass Apt., Lexington, KY
573.KCHO   Charlottesville-Albemarle, Charlottesville, VA
574.KGAI   Montgomery County Airpark, Gaithersburg, MD
575.KFXE   Fort Lauderdale Executive, Fort Lauderdale, FL
576.KTOL   Toledo Express, Toledo, OH
577.KBCT   Boca Raton Apt., Boca Raton, FL
578.KGGE   Georgetown CO. Apt., Georgetown, SC
579.KLRD   Laredo Int., Laredo, TX
580.KFMY   Page Field, Fort Myers, FL
581.KAUO   Auburn-Opelika Robert G Pitts, Auburn, AL
582.KBAZ   New Braunfels National Apt, New Braunfels TX
583.KTTN   Trenton Mercer, Trenton, NJ
584.KMFE   McAllen Miller Int., McAllen, TX
585.KCPS   St. Louis Downtown Apt., Cahokia/St. Louis, IL
586.K9A1   Covington Muni, Covington, GA
587.KM1J   Baldwin County
588.KAHN   Athens Ben Epps Apt., Athens, GA
589.KFDK   Frederick Muni, Frederick, MD
590.KVQQ   Cecil Field, Jacksonville, FL
591. 1A5   Macon County Apt., Franklin, NC
592.KISZ   Cincinnati Blue Ash, Cincinnati, OH
593.MYAT   Treasure Cay Abaco Island, Treasure Cay, BH
594.KFPR   St Lucie County Int., Fort Pierce, FL
595.KVHN   Culberson County, Van Horn, TX
596.KECP   NW Florida Beaches Int. Panama City, FL
597.KCEW   Bob Sikes Apt., Crestview, FL
598.KTMB   Miami Executive Apt., Miami, FL
599.X47   Flagler County, Bunnell, FL
600.KMSL   NW Alabama Regional, Muscle Shoals, AL
601.KSDF   Louisville Int.-Apt., Louisville, KY
602.KSRQ   Sarasota Bradenton Int., Sarasota-Bradenton, FL
603.KLYH   Lynchburg Regional-Apt., Lynchburg, VA
604.KMEZ   Mena Intermountain Muni, Mena, AZ
605.KBFM   Orlando Sanford Int., Orlando, FL
606.09J   Jekyll Island Apt., Jekyll Island, GA
607.KTIX   Space Coast Regional, Titusville, FL

608.KMTH   The Florida Keys Marathon Apt., Marathon, FL
609.KAWM   West Memphis Muni, West Memphis, AR
610.KCRX   Roscoe Turner, Corinth, MS
611.KOLV   Olive Branch Apt., Olive Branch, MS
612.KRUE   Russellville Regional, Russellville, AR
613.KIND   Indianapolis Int., Indianapolis, IN
614.KCAE   Columbia Metropolitan, Columbia, SC
615.KMKE   General Mitchell Int. Apt., Milwaukee, WI
616.KCPS   St Louis Downtown, Cahokia/St Louis, IL
617.KGNV   Gainesville Regional, Gainesville, FL
618.KEYW   Key West Int., Key West, FL
619.KPNS   Pensacola Regional, Pensacola, FL
620.KFYV   Drake Field, Fayetteville, AR
621.KSUS   Spirit of St Lewis, St Lewis, MO
622.KTIX   Space Coast Regional, Titusville FL
623.KMSN   Dane CO. Regional-Truax Field, Madison, WI
624.KMBO   Bruce Campbell Field, Madison, MS
625.KTHA   Tullahoma Regional/Northern, Tullahoma, TN
626.KGYY   Gary/Chicago Int., Gary, IN
627.KUVA   Garner Field, Uvalde, TX
628.TA34   Flying G (private), Crystal City, TX
629.KWW   West Woodward, Woodward, OK
630.KAEX   Alexandria Int., Alexandria, LA
631.KJWN   John C. Tune Apt., Nashville, TN
632.KESN   Easton/Newnan Field, Easton, MD
633.KMGM   Montgomery Regional, Montgomery, AL
634.KELM   Elmira/Corning Regional, Elmira/Corning, KY
635.KFYG   Washington Regional, Washington, MO
636.KMHE   Mitchell Muni, Mitchell, SD
637.KCVG   Cincinnati/North Kentucky Apt., Covington, KY
638.KSUA   Witham Field, Stuart, FL
639.95GA   McIntosh Field, Whitesburg, GA
640.KHMP   Atlanta Speedway Apt., Atlanta, GA
641.KGGG   East Texas Regional, Longview, TX
642.KPKB   Mid-Ohio Valley Regional, Parkersburg, WV
643.KHRO   Boone County Apt., Harrison, AR

644.KOMN   Ormond Beach Muni. Apt., Ormond Beach, FL
645.KN27   Bradford County Apt., Towanda, PA
646.KHLG   Wheeling Ohio County Apt., Wheeling, WV
647.KORF   Norfolk Int. Apt., Norfolk, VA
648.KEQY   Charlotte-Monroe Exe. Apt., Monroe, NC

649.K00A   Stone Mountain Apt., Stone Mtn. GA (Closed)

650.KPXE   Perry-Houston Apt.., Perry GA
651.KTRI   Tri-Cities Regional Apt.., Bristol, TN
652.KBKL   Raleigh County Memorial Apt., Beckley WV
653.KOWB   Owensboro-Davies County, Owensboro KY
654.KCRG   CRAIG Field, Jacksonville, FL
655.KCLE   Cleveland-Hopkins Int., Cleveland OH
656.KBKW   Raleigh County memorial Apt., Bleckley WV
657.KBLF   Mercer County Apt.., Bluefield, WV
658.K18A   Franklin County Apt.., Elberton GA
659.KAUB   Auburn University, Auburn AL
660.KAGC   Allegheny County Apt., Pittsburg, PA
661.KLMS   Louisville /Winston CO. Apt., Louisville, MS
662.KCSB   Cambridge Muni. Apt.., Cambridge NE
663.KSJC   Norman Y Mineta San Jose Int. Apt. San Jose CA
664.KPAQ   Palo Alto Airport, Palo Alto, CA
665.KSBO   Emanuel County Apt., Swainsboro, GA
666.9A5   Barwick Lafayette Apt., Lafayette, GA
667.KRKW   Rockwood Municipal Apt., Rockwood, TN
668.KDBN   W.H. Bud Barron Apt., Dublin, GA

669.4J2   Berrien CO. Apt, Nashville, GA
670.KLHW   Wright Army Field, Fort Stewart, GA
671.KEOE   Newberry CO. Apt., Newberry, SC
672.KMQY   Smyrna Apt., Smyrna, TN
673.KFYM   Fayetteville Apt., Fayetteville, TN
674.KCQF   HL Sonny Callahan Apt., Fairhope, AL
675.KMSY   New Orleans Int., New Orleans, LA

~

Some Celebrities Flown include - Michael Huckabee, Chipper Jones, Bret Michaels, John Travolta, David Gates, Jean Claude Killy, Beach Boys, Don Laughlin, Walter Hickel - Governor of Alaska, Bruce Babbitt - Secretary of the Interior, Days of our Lives TV Cast, and Hill Street Blues TV Cast.

Most famous Friend in Alaska

John Denver! Who came up almost every year.

Most famous Medevac was Garrett Bartelt. Flight from Valdez Alaska during Back Country Alaska I believe 1991.

The Nurses were extremely worried about this one. It seems he had an artery very close to the break in his leg.

https://www.youtube.com/watch?v=2o8_61pHLzQ

I damaged my right shoulder, slipped while standing on icy ramp holding my corner of the stretcher above my head, turning loose with one hand passing a syringe from one nurse to the other! Your Medevac job can be quite physical at times.

Most Famous Island – Single Pilot Conquest II

Attu, located approximately 1,700 miles from Anchorage, Alaska is the most remote island on the Aleutian Chain. I took the picture above after landing on the island on a rare, decent weather day. I had wandered up a small hill above the runway and discovered some ruins of battle. The island seemed to be a treasure-trove of WWII artifacts.

CHAPTER 12

WORK AND STUDY HISTORY

AVIATION EDUCATION / TRAINING:

1970 - 1975
MT. San Antonio College –
(Business - Commercial Aviation- Meteorology – Celestial Navigation)
Pomona Valley Aviation – Flight and Ground School
Attained:
Private Pilot's License
Commercial Pilot's License
Instrument Rating
Flight Instructor Rating
Multi-Engine Rating
Instrument Instructor Rating
Multi-Engine Instructor Rating
Passed DC 8 Flight Engineer Exams (.5 HRS Flt. DC8.)
(Passed California Real Estate Exam – Headed in that direction for a time as well as Flight Instructing.)
1976 Mobley's Aviation, Fulton CO. Airport, Atlanta, GA.
Attained: ATP License in BeechCraft Baron.
(4 Year Navy Veteran, Full time jobs, Family with Two Kids, evening classes at college, and flying on the weekends!)

It's hard but obviously can be done by just about anyone with Drive and Determination to move into a Flying Career.

You've just got to 'Go the Distance'!

JOURNEY PRIOR TO MY GENERAL AVIATION CAREER:

1959 – 1964 Sharpsburg, Georgia
Farm Work, Cabinet Shop
High School: Track Team, National Beta Club, President
Future Farmers of America, Honor Student
1964 - 1968
U.S. Navy – WESTPAC
Camp Nimitz, Basic Training, San Diego, California
USN A School, Electronics Tech, San Francisco, CA.
USS Vammen, Navy Destroyer, Long Beach, CA.
Marine Corp Combat/Survival TRN, Camp Pendleton, CA.
USN Seabees Training, Port Hueneme, CA.
USN MCB III, Naval Construction Battalion
(Attached to 3RDMarines Gia Le Combat Base)
Phu Bai, South Vietnam – (at Hue during 1968 Tet Offensive)
Awards - Two Letters of Commendation, Vietnam Service Medal w/ Marine Corp Insignia and one Star, Vietnam Campaign Medal, National Defense Service Medal, US Navy Sharpshooter, Secret Clearance, Honorable Discharge, Highest Rank - E-5
1968 – 1969 Atlanta, Georgia
Southern Bell Telephone -Installer/Repairman
1969 – 1975 Azusa, California –
Southern California Edison - Line Crew

I THINK THESE TWO ARE GREAT QUOTES FOR THOSE
WHO WISH TO GO THE DISTANCE...

This one sat on my desk in plain view for many years.

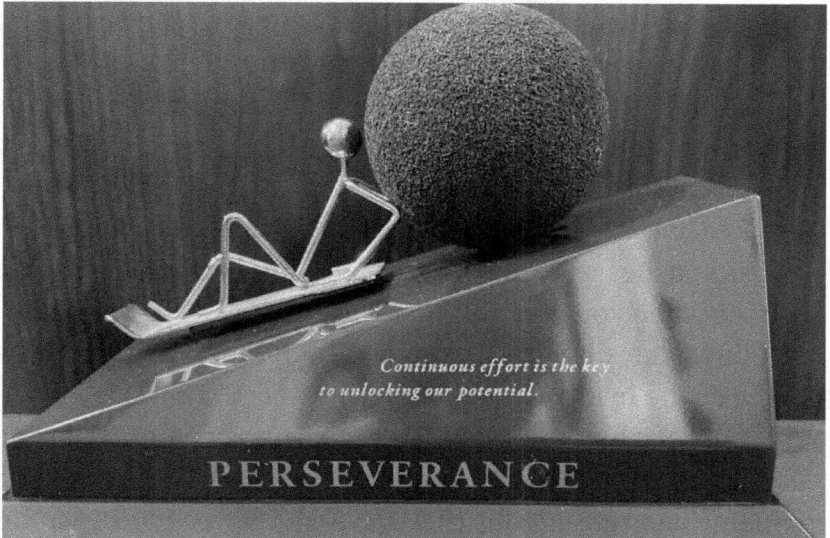

*Continuous effort is the key
to unlocking our potential.*

PERSEVERANCE

*Continuous Effort is the Key to Unlocking our
Potential*

*There Is No Chance, No Destiny, No Fate, That Can
Circumvent or Hinder or Control the Firm Resolve of
a Determined Soul. – Ella Wheeler Wilcox*

Hey, If I could do it, <u>YOU can do it!</u>

EPILOGUE

Through my long career and thousands of takeoffs and landings I've developed a strong Respect for the Engineers and Technicians that Designed and Built the machines we fly.

And, I have a strong Respect for the Mechanics and Technicians who have kept our machines flying.

Aviator's, Like Soldier's in the field there are hundreds of people that make our success possible.

So, be sure to Thank them in some way along the way.

In that awareness, you must realize that none of us accomplishes anything solely on our own although there are times when you may feel that way.

Consider all your Instructors, both Flight and Ground, as well as the Institutions that provide our Training.

Appreciate the F.A.A. for their oversight of and safety programs for the magnanimous Part 135 Charter type operations throughout the U.S. Also appreciate as well the N.T.S.B. for their study of accidents and finding out the reasons why.

Most of all you might want to appreciate some of the Aviation Giants who've gone before, explored, passed on their experiences and set precedents for others following in their footsteps. I certainly do.

U.S.S. Hornet Flight Deck with Lt. Colonel James Doolittle leading the way to Tokyo, Japan

Yes, Aviation Giants before even I was born!

Inspiration at a young age.

Lawrence Rainwater (My Uncle), U.S.N. Pacific 1942

Remember this picture hung on my grandfather's wall for years and inspired me at a very young age. Now that I think of it, the fact that he was a Sailor in the Navy may have unknowingly influenced me to sign up!

The Aviation end of it seems to have stuck with me as Later in Life, a Cousin, Jerry E. Blair took me to the Fulton County Airport in Atlanta, Georgia, sat me in a Cessna 150 Aircraft for the very first time and asked, "Tony, Do you think you can fly this thing?" I thought about it for a moment.

With the yoke in my hands, "I sure do Jerry!" – The rest is History... 29,000 Hours and 50 years later, Thank you Jerry!

You and others may have similar introductions to flying.

So,

Let's pass it on to the next generation.

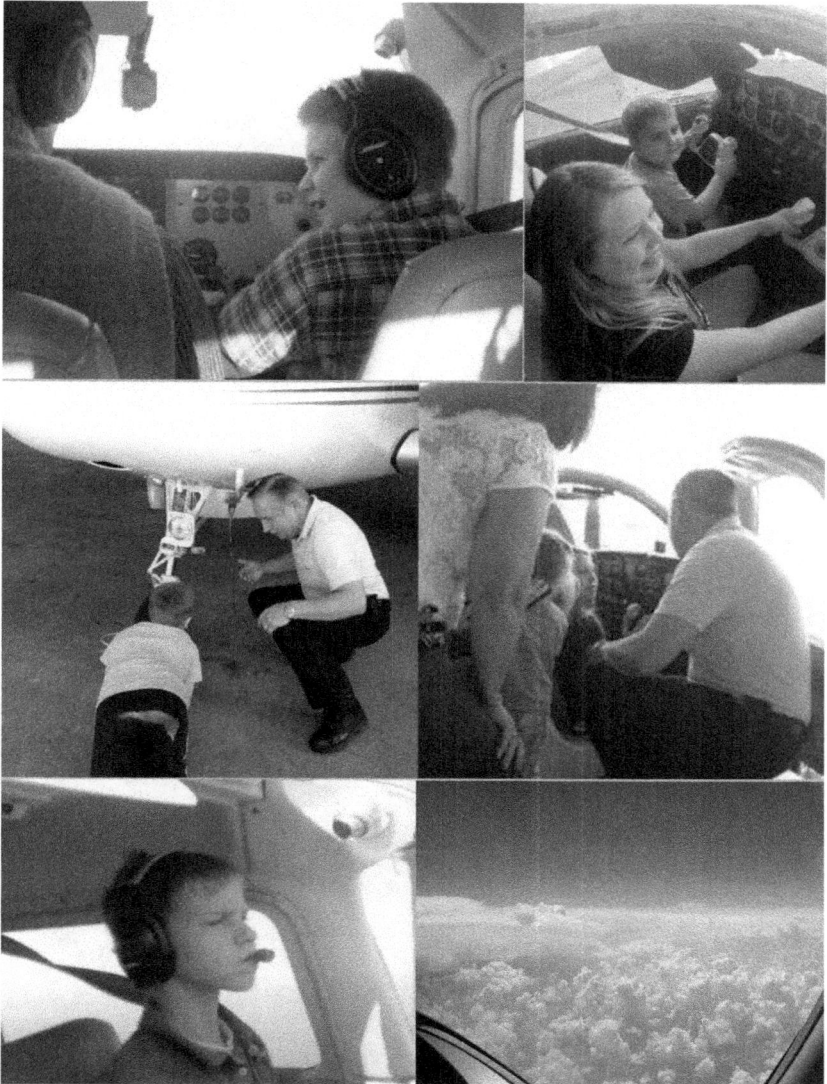

So, let's try to inspire them to take on this most challenging and amazing career!

Break their Surly Bond of Gravity as a Pilot

Or, Help them possibly consider Aviation in some other area of this vast industry.

CONCLUSION

As a Part 135 *On-Demand Charter Pilot*

YOU
   WILL
       <u>*NEVER*</u>
           RUN
               OUT
                   OF
                       STORIES TO TELL!

Blue Skies Ahead!

This Hand Woven Basket was given to me by Ruth, an Athabaskan Lady who was a regular Passenger living in Wales, Alaska. Really Great Folks!

This Awesome Colorado clock was constructed and given to me by one of my Excellent Students. First of mine to attain his Private Pilot License in 40 Hours! Thank you, Phil Dant!

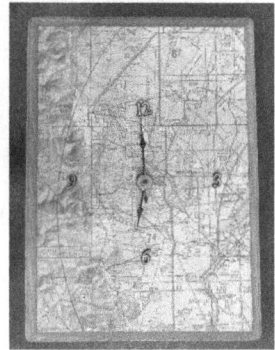

YOU CAN DO THIS!

AND THIS!

GOOD FLIGHTS. BLUE SKIES!

Other Great Aviation Books by this Author...
CALL SIGN SERIES plus
an Historical Novel 'Once a Warrior'

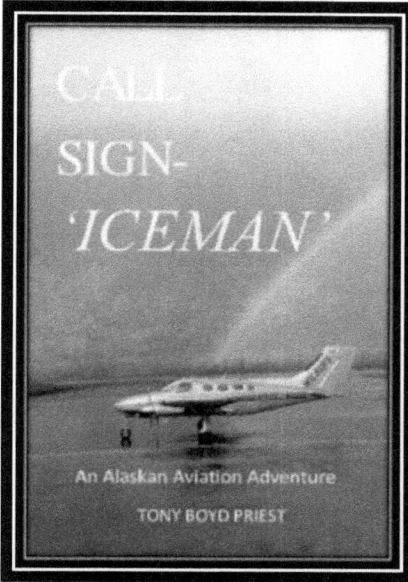

CALL SIGN- 'ICEMAN'
An Alaskan Aviation Adventure
TONY BOYD PRIEST

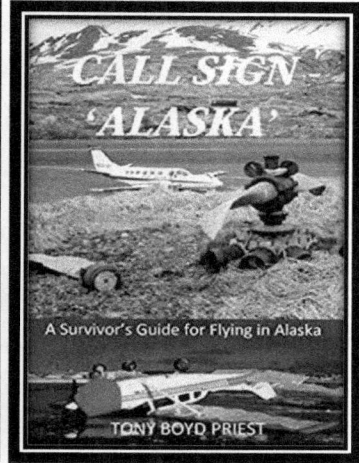

CALL SIGN - 'ALASKA'
A Survivor's Guide for Flying in Alaska
TONY BOYD PRIEST

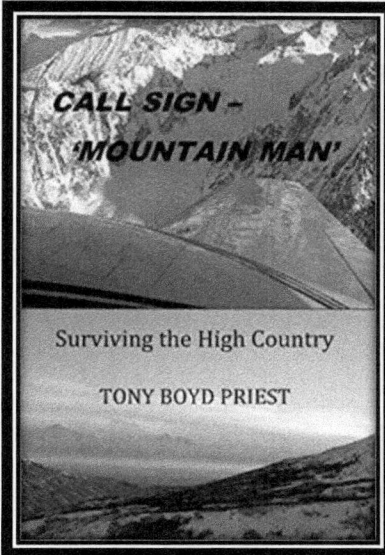

CALL SIGN - 'MOUNTAIN MAN'
Surviving the High Country
TONY BOYD PRIEST

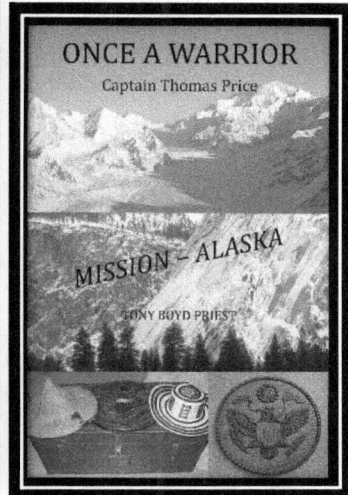

ONCE A WARRIOR
Captain Thomas Price
MISSION – ALASKA
TONY BOYD PRIEST